BARB,

in the

KINGDOM

Living a simple, purposeful and
passionate life for Christ

BARBARIANS
in the
KINGDOM

Living a simple, purposeful and
passionate life for Christ

Dan Swaningson

REDEMPTION
PRESS

Published by Redemption Press, PO Box 427, Enumclaw, WA 98022

Toll Free (844) 2REDEEM (273-3336)

Redemption Press is honored to present this title in partnership with the author. The views expressed or implied in this work are those of the author. Redemption Press provides our imprint seal representing design excellence, creative content, and high quality production.

ISBN 13: 978-1-68314-476-2 (Paperback)

Library of Congress Catalog Card Number: 2017955167

CONTENTS

INTRODUCTION

WHEN I FIRST did the series this book is based on for my church back in 2014, I struggled a bit with whether or not I should. I had contemplated it for a few years actually, ever since the earliest days of our church plant in Red Lodge, Montana, because I just *felt* like a barbarian; charging forth with little finesse and even less real direction, at least from man, when we started Hope Chapel. I knew in my spirit what I was supposed to do and, as those few who came with me know, we just made it happen—they even jokingly referred to us as *the barbarian church*. Fighting, it seemed, against even our own denomination who seemed intent at the time to make things as difficult as possible for us.

"Maybe we should just break free and be an independent 'barbarian church' . . . " Was the sentiment that the handful of brave souls that helped me plant the church only half-jokingly sometimes expressed in frustration. I knew I did not want to be out there without any covering or accountability so we stuck it out and kept paying our tribute to the ruling council in the motherland out west (to put it in barbarian terms)—and I'm glad we did. Our denomination has since gone through some major, God-ordained changes and things have gotten better, and much simpler, which was all I really wanted and what we all needed.

So anyway, the barbarian thing had been on my mind for some time but I just wasn't sure it was biblical. I mean, barbarians aren't usually thought of as exemplary citizens worthy of anything but disdain. What redeeming quality does a barbarian have that would make him a worthy topic for a sermon, let alone a series of sermons? Will people think I've lost it? Well, a couple of years ago, this son of the frozen barbarian north was fasting and praying about where I was to go next in my teaching and the Lord spoke to my heart, assuring me it was time to tackle the barbarian thing. As I prayed and sought the Lord further on this—"Really, how does that preach?" I wondered—he explained to me why it was important and showed me that it would *preach*.

The Holy Spirit opened my eyes to how it really does speak to who we are, why my own ministry exists, and where I believe the Spirit is directing his church. In a nutshell, back to the basics, to what's important. The Lord impressed on me three things—barbarian qualities—that exemplify why the kingdom needs barbarians to rise up and be heard in the church if it hopes to survive till the end.

The barbarian exemplifies:
Simplicity of purpose
Singularity of mission
Determination of spirit

It was this that convinced me that the church needed to hear this barbarian's message. I am glad I followed the Spirit's lead because this turned out to be one of the most empowering things we have done in our church as far as advancing the kingdom of God goes; lives were changed and hearts set free. So here we go again—this time with you along—storming the gates.

"Be strong, and let us fight bravely for our people and the cities of our God. The Lord will do what is good in his sight" (2 Sam. 10:12).

CHAPTER 1

The BARBARIAN with A BIBLE

I am a debtor both to Greeks and to barbarians. . . . (Rom. 1:14 NKJV)

SINCE THE VERY beginning of the church there have been barbarians in the kingdom. Many of the earliest battles were all about the simplicity of the gospel versus the complexity of religion—from Jesus with the Pharisees, and then Paul, the apostle to the Gentiles, against Peter who had originally brought the gospel to the dreaded Gentiles (much to the dismay of the new Jewish believers who sought to keep the law and all the religious ceremony and demands that went with that)—the most contentious battles of the early church were struggles against the simplistic straightforward notion that grace could just be claimed and held on to simply by tenaciousness and faith in something that couldn't be seen.

And that was the barbarian way in a nutshell. It was exactly what Jesus meant to bring to this world, but still we continue to complicate things. But let's not get ahead of ourselves—back to the beginning, when the barbarian was *appreciated* in the kingdom—at least by Paul.

"I am a debtor both to Greeks and to barbarians, both to wise and to unwise. So, as much as is in me, *I am* ready to preach the gospel to you who are in Rome also" (Rom. 1:14–15 NKJV).

"A debtor to the Greeks and the Barbarians." An interesting statement from the greatest theologian who ever lived, an apostle of Jesus Christ who recorded and explained the gospel in a way that the western Greek-influenced mind could understand, using the reason and philosophical models first shaped and applied by the Greeks.

Paul coupled this style of reasoning with the boldness and dogged determination exemplified by the barbarians, who also demanded things be simple and straightforward. Paul became a master at both reason and simplicity: "For I resolved to know nothing while I was with you except Jesus Christ and him crucified." (1 Cor. 2:2). Yet he also laid out the case in such an intricate and all-encompassing way that two thousand years later we are still marveling at the depth and subtleties of his teaching.

"To them God has chosen to make known among the Gentiles the glorious riches of this mystery, which is Christ in you, the hope of glory. He is the one we proclaim, admonishing and teaching everyone with all wisdom, so that we may present everyone fully mature in Christ" (Col. 1:27–28).

The barbarians, those who had resisted first the Greek, and then the Latin influence, grabbed ahold of the gospel and ran with it—the *mystery* revealed in Jesus Christ—while the eastern mind, befuddled with mysticism and riddles, continued to overthink it. Yet we mostly ignore the barbarian thing that Paul seems to be putting on equal footing with the Greeks and we all strive to be the Greeks. As a result, we become too smart for our own good. We outsmart ourselves right out of the simplicity of not just life in general, but the gospel as well.

Not me—I have come to embrace and even appreciate my inner barbarian. I spent too many years trying to play the game—man's game—with all the rules made by people I always assumed were smarter than I, only to discover that in the end it must be God I seek first *and* last. I'm talking about the church, the politics and hierarchies we set up with good intentions, but if we are not careful and diligent they only get in the way of our following the master—Jesus Christ.

What is this barbarian you speak of?

"Barbarian with a Bible." I told my church shortly after we started, that I was simply a "barbarian with a Bible." It just seemed to fit what I was talking about at the time—me being a simple man with a simple message—and it kind of stuck. It just keeps coming back around. A lot of folks get a kick out of that—some more than others—and it's always good for a laugh, but most don't realize that I am plumb serious. In fact, the Lord himself, a couple of years ago, started calling me a barbarian as an affirmation of who he wanted me to be. We'll get back to that story later.

To me, the name barbarian may have a different meaning than it does to others. It's often used in a derogatory fashion and indeed that is the origin of the word. It comes from the Latin word *barbarus*—Latin being the language of ancient Rome—referring to those who lived north of the Empire; the untamed, uncivilized tribes living in the northern forests and grassy steppes of Europe. Of course, they were untamed and uncivilized in the minds of the mighty Roman empire mainly because they had not allowed themselves to be conquered by the Romans; the Germanic tribes, the Franks, the Celts, the Goths and Visigoths, the Gauls, the Huns—to name a few. Some of them were eventually subjugated by the Romans, but those who managed to stay free would become Rome's undoing as Rome became overextended, overreaching, and self-absorbed.

While the Romans were busy playing their games of politics and immersing themselves in every kind of debauchery, the barbarians were pressing back at the ever-expanding frontiers, eventually reversing the tide and finally storming the gates of Rome itself. Their mission of survival and conquest, steeled by a single-minded determination to put an end to the oppression and terror, the tyranny they had lived under or been threatened by for generations—overcame the most powerful empire the world had ever known.

Unfortunately, this total overthrow of all things Roman also threw the world into the dark ages as much of the world's knowledge and technology was either destroyed or forgotten by those who only sought out gold, weapons, and food, while destroying the rest. Being a barbarian in this "eat, drink and be merry" kind of mindset—gratifying only the desires of the flesh—is surely not the noblest of claims. Any group of people living in their basest state apart from the true God can quickly become *savage* and uncaring, devaluing all life other than their own.

I shudder when I hear of modern Muslim extremists referred to as "barbaric," as they have been in the news lately, when they behead people or enslave women and children. That's not barbarism, that's cowardice and savagery—just plain evil. Historically, yes, barbarians could be savage, and they often were; but so can any group of people, even the *civilized*. If beating people in the streets and burning police cars and businesses because your candidate lost an election is the way a civilized society expresses an opinion, then the civilized are highly overrated. Then there is the tearing apart of an unborn child in the sanctuary of the womb; that is as savage as it gets, yet our civilized society embraces it and protects this act as a Constitutional right.

This son of barbarians would like to thump some heads together and say "Wake up, people! We are destroying our own neighborhoods and killing our own children, sacrificing them on the altar of convenience, and we will have to answer to the God who created those lives." Abortion is not a political issue—it is life and death and this country is being sold a bill of goods that is not just killing babies, but is leaving a trail of brokenhearted young women who will spend the rest of their lives trying to deal with the pain and condemnation that *inevitably* catches up with them. The truth can only be held back so long.

I don't think head thumping is the answer, but sometimes I wonder. Then I look in my Bible and it says to love them; only when they feel accepted by the truth will they accept the truth.

Anyway, back to the dark ages

Speaking of truth being held back. The dark ages were just that, all of western civilization living in the darkness of ignorance, starving for truth. Ironically, it was another group, who became known as barbarian, that was instrumental in rescuing the western world from those dark days of ignorance and superstition; the Vikings, another untamed tribe of uncivilized barbarians living in the frozen north country, who would swoop down and raid the people who, a few hundred years earlier, were doing the same to the, by then, long-dead Roman empire.

By then Europe was caught in the grip of the feudal system, living in squalor as peasants; controlled and used basically as slave labor and soldiers at the whim of a few very wealthy people—the nobles, who controlled all wealth and land. But even they served an even higher power; the church, the final (yet powerful) vestige of the Roman Empire—the Holy Roman church, holding the power of heaven and hell to be dispensed at their will, often to manipulate and embezzle.

Then along come the Vikings, raiding, burning, and killing. Free men who bowed down to no one, taking what they wanted with ferocious and terrifying efficiency, striking out of nowhere and disappearing again on the waves of the sea in their dragon-headed longships that would come to be the stuff of nightmares for generations. "Save us, O Lord, from the wrath of the Norseman!"—A prayer on the lips of many for generations.

The Vikings' prime targets were those very same churches who had themselves pillaged an entire populace using the threat of hell like a double-edged sword. Their imposing high-steepled churches and their monasteries—where all the wealth they had absconded with was hoarded—were easy pickings for those who answered to no one, certainly not to those who called themselves priests of some foreign God. They had no respect or fear for this bunch of soft-bellied weak-limbed men, whose hands craved the feel of gold but blanched at the steel of the sword hilt. Men who had never torn their hands pulling on an oar, yet worshiped a God whose flesh had been ripped to shreds by the so called *civilized*.

But as these easy targets began to be fewer and farther between, these freebooting barbarians began to see that there was more money to be had—a better lot for their families and a much better chance of going home at the end of an adventure—if they turned their energies to trading. Thus they became the first to tie the world back together after centuries of fracture; the east to the west, England to France and Germany, Russia to Constantinople.

They discovered new lands in the west—Greenland, Iceland, and Vinland—and established trade routes between them and Ireland, Scotland, and Wales, even building port cities such as Dublin, York, Kiev, and Reykjavik, which still thrive today. Suddenly Bagdad and Constantinople could trade with Iceland, Greenland, and Vinland and all points in between. Isolated, dark corners of the world, where people had only heard legends and fables of other faraway places, became international hubs for trade as those longships they once feared carried goods, news, and people from exotic places they never dreamed existed, let alone could be traded with.

Because of a bunch of barbarians, the world became a much smaller place, as the Scandinavians became the distributers of the world's wealth and resources. Languages and information were shared across the world, the lost wisdom of the ages, of Socrates and Plato, ferreted away in the quickly shrinking Byzantine empire of the east, was once again sparking a desire, and laying the groundwork, for all of Europe and the Middle East to once again seek out and understand that there is an order and a science to this world we live in; that an intelligent God did create this world to be a good and just place for us to live.

Because the barbarians rocked the boat and broke down the barriers, the world began to see that there was so much more to this world—to this life—than just surviving another day. That man could achieve and improve his lot, and lo and behold, the Renaissance happened, followed closely by the Reformation and of course the Christianization of those Viking barbarians as they put away the sword of conquest in favor of the living sword—the Bible. Yet the conquest continued.

Once those barbarians got ahold of the truth, there was another revolution as the Germans, Saxons, and Celts, the Brits, French, and Scandinavians—and so on—sought out and fought for their right to worship their God; to live as free men and women who could work hard, pray harder, and live the life they chose while benefiting from the fruits of their own labor.

All of this culminated and found its truest expression in the land and country called America, the land of the free and the home of the brave, extending across a continent first seen as a cold and unwelcoming distant land by those barbarian raiders and traders almost 500 hundred years before the first civilized Christian ever knew it existed; the land once called Vinland and inhabited by another race of barbarians that the Vikings had decided to let have the land. The Vikings called them Skraeling—wild men. Columbus would call them Indians. At least the Vikings were smart enough to know they weren't in India.

The spirit of the barbarian

So when I talk about myself being a barbarian, it's the spirit of adventure and courage, the desire to make things happen, to advance and enhance whatever agenda I have determined is worthy of my efforts, no matter what or who would try to stop me, that I aspire to. I know my ancestry and that I am descended from many of those northern tribes once called barbarian. Primarily the Scandinavian, Dutch, Irish, and English all delightfully mixed together in me and deposited here today in the middle of Montana as a sort of barbarian smoothie.

But remember the rest of that—I am a "barbarian with a Bible." Meaning that barbarian propensity towards getting it done, making it happen—that "I have made up my mind and you had better not get in my way" spirit of freedom—is tempered and directed by the black and white, "this is right and this is wrong"—laws of my God *and* by the Spirit of truth that lives within my heart, and I no longer live and fight to gratify the desires of the flesh, but my energies are now expended towards living for the Spirit and advancing his kingdom—and you still had better not in get in my way.

No doubt many of you are descendants of some of those barbarians as well, and you have that same heritage and spirit. In reality, pretty much *every race* and people has a barbarian past, some older, some more recent. The ones north of Rome just happen to be the ones who got the name "Barbarian." I believe that deep within the heart of every person is the desire for a straightforward, "Don't mess with me or mine and we'll be fine, tell me no lies and I'll trust you with my life and give mine for you," kind of spirit.

And when focused, empowered, and tempered by the truth of God's Word and by the living Word—Jesus Christ—we—the church, the Gentiles grafted into the kingdom to share in the inheritance first promised to the descendants of Abraham—are unstoppable, uncontainable, and will not be deterred—unless we choose to allow ourselves to be. And that is what this book is all about: learning to storm the gates of hell, set the captives free from their chains of slavery imposed on them by nobles and priests, and knowing when to stop, throw up our visors, wipe the sweat off our brows, and glory in the simple pleasures of the sun on our faces, the cool breeze in our hair, and the camaraderie of our brothers and sisters in arms.

I believe that is why the Lord led me to teach on what it means to be a barbarian in the kingdom of God and why the kingdom needs us barbarians. The church has forgotten the fulfillment and the pure joy of victory that is to be had in fighting and winning the *right* battles, the simple pleasures of a life of freedom and the importance of defending it. The church has enough politicians and philosophers; it's time to take hold of the life to which we were called; to fight the good fight fearlessly and wholeheartedly.

> "Fight the good fight of the faith. Take hold of the eternal life to which you were called when you made your good confession in the presence of many witnesses. In the sight of God, who gives life to everything" (1 Tim. 6:12–13).

I needed a barbarian

I told you earlier the Lord had called me to be the barbarian; here's the rest of the story. It had to do with our fight to get into a building where we had a little more elbow room and parking than our downtown storefront did. Those who were around in those early days of our church know what a challenge that was, as building after building seemed to elude us. I spent much of nearly every weekend driving and walking around Red Lodge looking for a suitable place. It was a real challenge, with very little money, but I was determined. I told my wife, Donna, that I felt like a stalker; always stalking one building or another and their owners. One of the more promising opportunities that came along was an old funeral chapel. It was a ready-made church, just add people. The owner was a family friend but he wasn't interested in leasing it—he wanted to sell. As an "unchartered" church at the time, we were not allowed to purchase property under our denominational rules. Until we had thirty official members we were considered a plant and could only lease, and even then only with approval from the suits in Los Angeles. The owner offered to do a contract for deed, kind of like a rent to own deal. Quandary: It seemed like a workable deal; the building had ample room, plenty of parking, room for kids—it was even furnished—but I knew it would be nearly impossible to get this through our denomination heads. In my talking to them about this it was also discovered that they had lost track of five months' worth of our tithe checks to them. So we were not even qualified to lease, let alone buy, until we proved we had tithed. I was determined to do things by the book but the book was not cooperating.

Needless to say, I was getting very frustrated. So I prayed, and I prayed hard. Here is how the Lord answered me and the reason I have embraced my inner barbarian. I have a journal entry dated April 4, 2012, that reads: "I sent you to Red Lodge because I needed a barbarian, not a politician—to get things done, to storm the gates. Go with the program till the program gets in the way and then step over it. There are people that need healing, real hurts and heartaches, don't let anything stop you from following me." The Spirit was telling me to follow Jesus, not a rule book!

That changed my whole perspective on ministry. I was not here to placate and glorify my denomination, nor Hope Chapel, nor myself. I am not here to avoid stepping on toes and make everyone like me; I am here because Jesus asked me to be here and I will follow him no matter what the voices of those who think I am doing it wrong say. I am here to advance the kingdom of God, offer healing and hope to those who have been wounded in the war, and make a place for those who *want* to join the Lord's army—an army of barbarians who know what we know; Jesus is Lord, he is my King and commander, and neither of those things is open for debate—plain and simple.

We did not get that building; at the last minute the owner decided we were not in a position to buy. But I had a new resolve to be ready for the building the Lord did have for us and after a couple of other possibilities fell through, this place we are now in came available and we jumped on it. Long story short, the Lord just opened one door after another to get us in here, sometimes before we had even knocked. And just five months after I had called the owner and told him we were interested in the building, we had gutted the building, remodeled, and had Easter service there.

Just before we moved in I called the district office, in Missoula at that time, to tell them that we were " . . . renting a new building, had remodeled it without borrowing a dime, and were about to move in"—long pause—"Does LA know about this?" "Nope, we had to move fast, property in Red Lodge does not wait for bureaucracy."

A month or so after we moved in I got official permission from LA to rent the building. This barbarian and his church found it all very amusing; this is indeed God's church.

"I desire to do your will, my God; your law is within my heart" (Ps. 40:8).

The Lord gave me this verse as I was originally pondering this series, still wondering if it was indeed the right thing to do. When I read this, it hit me like a ton of bricks—or a barrel full of *Lutefisk*—that the barbarian mindset is one of simplicity of purpose. That is exactly what my ministry is all about and where I believe the Spirit is trying to redirect his church. In the chapters to come we'll look more at what this really means and how we live it out. I have a simple unwritten mantra for my ministry approach—unwritten because it doesn't look good on a church bulletin—"Keep it simple, stupid." The barbarian epitomizes simplicity.

We need to be able to—and allow others to—live, love, and laugh. We need to approach life with a single-minded "get it done, make it happen" sense of mission. Life is too short to do otherwise. And we need to remember that if it's worth having, it's worth fighting for—to attain or to keep. Simple rules to live by.

Be the barbarian

The barbarian is comfortable with who they are; the civilized sophisticate does not intimidate him or her. They are unashamed and unapologetic about their passionately and deeply held beliefs. "I am not ashamed of the gospel of Christ . . . " (Rom. 1:16).

It's the simplicity of a walk with Jesus. Uncluttered by religion, hang-ups, codependent fears, and demands. The voice that would hinder or discourage, the voices of the past that told you that you could not, will not, and are not worthy to accomplish or be who you know deep down inside that you are supposed to be; what you are supposed to do. Those things must be trodden over like the manure in the pasture that you have to step over to get to the war stallion that awaits you if you are simply brave enough to answer the call and to move in the conviction of your soul where the Spirit of the Lord who has been compelling you to action and freedom is just waiting to hand you the reins and point you in the direction of your mission unhindered by politics, red tape, and lawyers.

It is my mission, the mission of my ministry, and the purpose of this writing to turn you out a warrior, whole and healed from past battles where you were overwhelmed because you were underfed, uninspired, and expected to fight in several battles simultaneously without even engaging in the battle that was tugging at your heart the most. The war is being lost because we are all fighting the wrong battles, or too many without reprieve, and getting wounded, exhausted, and left behind. It is our command to end this travesty, to show the church what it means to follow Jesus as free men; barbarians fighting for the kingdom, not as mercenaries but as volunteers who love their King and have one desire—*to do his will!*

> "Be strong, and let us fight bravely for our people and the cities of our God. The Lord will do what is good in his sight" (2 Sam. 10:12).

CHAPTER 2

SIMPLICITY OF PURPOSE

Indeed, when Gentiles, who do not have the law, do by nature things required by the law, they are a law for themselves, even though they do not have the law. They show that the requirements of the law are written on their hearts. . . . (Rom. 2:14–15)

I CONTEND THAT Barbarism is a state of mind, one the kingdom needs—as long as it is a state of mind that is subject to Christ. As we saw earlier, the name *barbarian* was originally a term used to designate a group of people: those unconquered and uncivilized tribes living north of the mighty Roman empire. In later centuries those now "civilized" barbarians would reassign this term to reference the Norsemen who would pour out of the north, taking what they wanted and answering to no one. We now know them as Vikings. The sword and the battle ax was their law—at least in regard to the world outside of their own communities.

Within their villages and clans they did live by a code of conduct, a strict and honorable code of conduct that honored and protected women and children and ensured that all could live in security and that they each had a voice. Within this codified culture, as in nearly all barbarian cultures, the women had an equal voice and were respected. Many of them fought alongside the men in battle and some even led men in battle; hence the venerated shield maidens—a misnomer, as according to the Norse sagas they did much more than hold shields and bat their eyes; they led warriors from the front.

The lower class?

It's really a notion that comes along with civilization, advanced learning, and religious regulations, that the women should be subjugated and diminished to a lower class of citizen. We saw that in ancient Israel—a very patriarchal culture—and in our own country's not-so-ancient history. Until just a few generations ago, women couldn't even vote, and if they chose to work outside of the house their options were few as they were relegated to being nurses, teachers, waitresses, or secretaries. We now see that religious expression of female subjugation to the extreme in much of Islam where, under Sharia law, women are little more than livestock.

God has an answer to that: "There is neither Jew nor Greek, there is neither slave nor free, there is neither male nor female; for you are all one in Christ Jesus" (Gal. 3:28 NKJV).

Paul reiterates this to the Colossians: " . . . and have put on the new man who is renewed in knowledge according to the image of Him who created him, where there is neither Greek nor Jew, circumcised nor uncircumcised, barbarian, Scythian, slave nor free, but Christ is all and in all" (Col. 3:10–11 NKJV).

There is no room for the subjugation or devaluing of anyone in God's kingdom, and again we see the barbarian put on an equal footing with the "oh so philosophical" Greek and the spiritual and meticulously pious Jew. Everyone—man, woman, slave, and free—is equal in the kingdom of God among those who put their hope in Christ. So again I ask the question. Why do we strive to emulate the "Greek" and the "Jew"—the sophisticated and the religious?—"Let's debate and argue theology until we don't even remember what the debate is about anymore, and let's see how many more rules and rituals we can cram into our written, and unwritten, personal books of do's and don'ts until we get so caught up in the doing, so hung up in the nuances of our theological bents, that we forget what the purpose of it all was in the first place."— that we can no longer see the forest for the trees.

According to this scripture, there is no advantage to being one over the other, for our identity is now in Christ. The woman should not strive and desire to be like the man. The Greek should not try to become the Jew; the barbarian should not try to emulate—to try to act like someone they are not—as though we must fit into a certain mold; "I must be sophisticated and highly educated like the Greek. I have to be a shining example of religious perfection like the God-fearing Jew—always seeking . . . " The point is, *be who you are!* That's what this is saying.

If you are of the barbarian persuasion—then be the barbarian! That is the simplicity of purpose. You cannot spend your life trying to be someone you are not. If you commit yourself to Christ *as* a barbarian and he welcomes you into his arms of love, then be the best barbarian for Christ that you can be. He loved and called you for who you are. It's hard enough to keep the flesh at bay and try to keep the Spirit prevalent in our hearts—we don't need to make it all but impossible by trying to be someone we are not. Playing yourself in the drama of life is much simpler than playing someone else—someone you wish you were, or were told you must be.

I'm not picking on the Jew or the Greek or even the mysterious Scythian; they are just representative of different types of thoughts—the variety that is needed in the kingdom—and that's what the Scripture is saying; these groups are just representative of different schools of thought, different personalities and backgrounds. None is better than any other—whether it's race, gender, social position, or culture—so don't try to be something you are not.

So back to why we need barbarians in the kingdom and what we can learn from them:

As I said at the start, barbarism is a state of mind and the barbarian's mindset in the kingdom is one of simplicity of purpose, "Make it happen, appreciate the right, destroy the wrong, and don't waste time with things that in the end don't matter." The barbarian mind is a free mind, one that is uncluttered by the civilized and learned notions of what's important. He doesn't fret over the temporal; he doesn't play games and worry about the latest political correctness agenda item because he doesn't need someone else to tell him what's right and wrong. He doesn't need someone else to tell him how to think—or not think. The barbarian default mode of common sense practicality *is* the operative mode, making life much simpler *and* sustainable.

I have to confess that I love reading the old Conan stories by Robert E. Howard—the original creator of the world's most famous fictional barbarian. Howard created Conan as a man unfettered by the whims and complications of civilization. He was pretty black and white—uncomplicated. He lived for the thrill of adventure and the lure of gold, but in his quests for either, he was always having to save a damsel in distress, rescue the innocent from some evil sorcerer, and defend the defenseless. In the Conan sagas, brute strength, common sense, a sharp sword, and a barbarian's instinct always won the day—a refreshing departure from our own reality.

I saved this quote from a Conan story a few years ago for just such an occasion as this: "'Barbarism is the natural state of mankind,' the borderer said, still staring somberly at the Cimmerian. 'Civilization is unnatural. It is a whim of circumstance. And barbarism must always ultimately triumph.'" —Robert E. Howard, Conan the Barbarian, "Beyond the Black River."

Obviously that's not Scripture, but it speaks to the heart of what I'm getting at here. If we look deep inside and discover who we are, who God created us to be, and are striving to let that person thrive and survive, we will ultimately triumph. We are created in the image of God, we are created by God and renewed by his Holy Spirit as believers. Why would we try to be someone we are not? Why would we try to *civilize and structure* our lives—change our inner person—to be socially acceptable according to whatever the majority of those around us are assimilating themselves to.

One day everything may come crashing down and all we have left is who we are—we had better know who we are. You have to know what's in your heart. The barbarian with a Bible has the *truth* written on his or her heart, the place they have always gone seeking truth, the heart, guided by a nobleness of purpose, an ear tuned to those they love and to what their hearts are saying. They are not weighed down by a lot of complicated rules and traditions that have lost their meaning long ago. In the barbarian's heart common sense is still common.

The law on the heart

God never intended for us to become so caught up in the doing, spending our energies trying to please him with things that are no longer connected to our hearts—let alone anyone else's. Even under the old covenant of the law, God took issue with this religious spirit that was taking the place of a simple, purposeful relationship to God and His Word. "Sacrifice and offering you did not desire—but my ears you have opened—burnt offerings and sin offerings you did not require. Then I said, 'Here I am, I have come—it is written about me in the scroll. I desire to do your will, my God; your law is within my heart'" (Ps. 40:6–8).

This is a Messianic prophecy . . . that the Messiah would come and exemplify what it meant to have the Word written on the heart—to want to do the will of God—not just keeping the letter of the law but the *spirit* of the law. The law was intended to bring life. Instead, mankind in his formulaic wisdom, decided it was more important to go through all the right motions—that it was easier to have a rule book than a relationship. But Jesus came along and changed all that—at least for those who would listen.

"I desire to do your will, my God; your law is within my heart." That has to be our mindset as well—"I *desire* to do your will—I want to live your ways, to fulfill the purpose that you have for me in the way that you want me to fulfill it. I want it to become a part of me, just like breathing; that the intent of the law, to 'love the Lord your God with all your heart and love your neighbor as yourself,' becomes a very part of my character. I love and live for God and my fellow man because it's who I am; it's what I want to do, not because I am trying to earn brownie points with God that will hopefully add up to a blessing somewhere along the line."

The Barbarian mindset is one of simplicity—simplicity of purpose—the purpose being to live a life that matters. One that matters because it made this world a better place for those around it. What a contrast to the selfishness of the world and to those with a religious spirit. "He has made us competent as ministers of a new covenant—not of the letter but of the Spirit; for the letter kills, but the Spirit gives life" (2 Cor. 3:6).

We are the ministers of the new covenant—the one now written on our hearts. There is no place there for selfishness, not if our hearts are truly guided by the Spirit of God, a heart motivated only by love—love for God and love for others—a heart that appreciates the beauty of all those things.

Jesus, the Barbarian Messiah

When I think of simplicity of purpose I think of Jesus. He had one basic purpose and he did it with what I told you before were the three basic tenets of the barbarian mindset: "Simplicity of purpose, singularity of mission, and determination of spirit."

He indeed had a *singular mission*; his mission was to remove anything that would hinder us from a relationship with his Father. He had a *determination* that emanated from his very soul—nothing was going to stop him, not even death—a determination of spirit. And he could tell you without hesitation what his *purpose* was in a simple and straightforward way: "The Son of man came to seek and to save the lost" (Luke 19:10).

That's simplicity of purpose. People were lost because they had let things get in the way of their relationship with God; initially it was sin, but the more they tried to find ways to deal with it, the more complicated it got and the farther and farther God seemed to be. Then along comes Jesus, the unsophisticated construction worker from way up north acting the barbarian.

He shows up in Jerusalem and he does the unthinkable: He walks into the temple courtyard in the height of the Passover week and starts wreaking havoc among the vendors who have set up their tables, pens, and tills—all according to standing tradition, and with the blessing of the temple priests. No doubt they paid dearly for their spaces to set up and make their money from the religious pilgrims who have come from all over the empire to make their sacrifices in the temple of their God.

Jesus comes in—apparently not just once, but on two different Passovers—and throws over the tables of the money changers, tables covered with coins from all over the Roman Empire that had to be exchanged for the Jewish shekel so that people could pay the temple tax. Imagine the looks of shock, disbelief, and anger on the faces of those who had been carefully stacking and stashing their coins, as the coins go flying across the paving stones amongst the feet of hundreds of people. But Jesus doesn't stop there; he then drives them out of the courtyard using a whip he had previously knotted together from cords; probably the ropes used to lead in the animals that were being sold to the pilgrims right there in the temple courtyard, the same animals he would turn loose from their holding pens and also drive from the temple.

Why? Why did he act so radically? Because this carnival of greed and chaos was taking place in the one place on earth where common people were supposed to, and were able to, come before their God— his Father—and worship him in his presence. Jesus had come to seek and to save the lost. The lost *were* lost because they were prevented from being in the presence of a Holy God by their sin. And the one place on earth where there was hope of finding absolution—the place where a sinner could come into the proximity of God and have his or her prayers for deliverance and forgiveness heard—was cluttered to the point where the last thing anyone could do was pray. "It is written," he said to them. "'My house will be a house of prayer'; but you have made it a den of robbers" (Luke 19:46).

Interestingly, it was the court of the Gentiles—the barbarian court—that Jesus was so passionate about uncluttering that day. This was the only part of the temple where the non-Jewish person was allowed to go, the part of the temple where the Gentile could pray. Apparently the religious were unconcerned with the barbarian, or the Greek, or the Roman—or anyone else for that matter. The religious are only concerned for themselves, *What can I get out of this and how will this make me look good?* But Jesus was concerned with people; that was his purpose, his mission, and he would stop at nothing to accomplish it—straightforward and simple, "You get in the way of my mission, we are going to have a problem, and I *will* make this happen!"

At first blush, this sounds unloving but Jesus had little patience for those whose hearts were full of greed and religion because they hindered and harmed more people than anyone else—people he loved. There is nothing more harmful to the kingdom than a religious person (yes, I just said that) because they are the ones pretending to know God while claiming to hold the keys. The tax collectors and sinners that Jesus was accused of fraternizing with never pretended to be righteous or to have it all figured out; they deceived no one. These religious and greedy people in the temple were stealing eternity from those Jesus was sent to save, and he was not going to tolerate it; he was not going to negotiate or play games. He knew what he had to do and he did it—body, soul, and mind—driven by a single, passionate purpose.

That is the same approach Jesus took when he faced the cross.

The barbarian mindset that I believe we are being asked to embrace—the one that Jesus illustrated by his life and death—is one that is straightforward, simple, and focused. Simplicity of purpose is simply being straightforward, simple, and focused. That is what the barbarian brings to the kingdom, and that is what we need. It's getting back to basics, back to your first love. The Jesus you first met and loved was the one who just said, "Come to me and I will heal and forgive, and make you whole. I have a plan for you, just for you, and I will never leave you nor forsake you." Then we lose sight, Jesus gets shrouded in mystery, complicated theologies and demands. And we just stop following. Who cut in on you to keep you from obeying the truth? "The only thing that counts is faith expressing itself through love. You were running a good race. Who cut in on you to keep you from obeying the truth?" (Gal. 5:6b–7).

We must not get sidetracked; we need to finish the race. Whatever it is that the Lord has put on your heart, whatever he has given you the gifts and the talents to do, whatever your passion is—that is what you need to be doing. This life is too short to play games; God put you here for a time such as this. He put you where you are for a reason and he gave you a brain; he gave you the Holy Spirit—the one Jesus called the Counselor—and he gave you his written Word to make sure you would not be deceived.

Don't let anyone cut in on you and stop you. You have to be focused. If you do that—keep it simple and keep moving straight ahead without all the side trips, distractions, and detours—you will finish the race, and you will accomplish your mission. You will not be so easily burned out, exhausted, and discouraged if you live your life this way. The church is full of wounded warriors—the wounded warrior is the one who was in the wrong place at the wrong time. Jesus will never lead you to the wrong place.

Jesus kept it simple

Jesus knew his mission. He had people pulling him every which way, but he was focused. He had voices from every side telling him, "Go this way, go that way, don't go there—don't say that!" "Be our king." "Tell your disciples to be quiet." "Don't insult the Pharisees." "Come quick, my brother is sick—if you had been here he wouldn't have died." "I'll never let them take you, I'll never deny you" But his response was always, as best said in the garden on that fateful night, "Father, . . . not my will, but yours be done" (Luke 22:42).

His mission wasn't simple to accomplish, but it was simple to explain and understand because he knew exactly what it was and that he could only accomplish it by listening to and obeying his Father and by being who he was—straightforward, simple, and determined. Because of his obedience and dogged determination, we are free; because of his single-minded, "get it done no matter what it takes" barbarian-like focus and simplicity of purpose, even we barbarians are now welcome and embraced in the kingdom of his Father. Barbarians in the kingdom—living, loving, and laughing. Living hard, fighting hard, and loving harder.

Follow your gut

"Indeed, when Gentiles, who do not have the law, do by nature things required by the law, they are a law for themselves, even though they do not have the law. They show that the requirements of the law are written on their hearts, their consciences also bearing witness, and their thoughts sometimes accusing them and at other times even defending them" (Rom. 2:14–15).

Barbarians would call this following your gut.

The law is written on our hearts. We instinctively know what is right and what is wrong. A barbarian who has made Jesus his Lord does not need to be led around by the hand and harangued by uppity preachers to know when something is wrong or what is right. We don't have to have the Hollywood elite or the ACLU tell us what the latest thing is we are supposed to be indignant about or suddenly okay with; the ever-changing cause of the day is not our great concern because we have an eternal truth—the living Word—not just written, but living within our hearts.

And we are not ashamed of it. "For I am not ashamed of the gospel, because it is the power of God that brings salvation to everyone who believes: first to the Jew, then to the Gentile" (Rom. 1:16). Political correctness never saved anyone. Political correctness and trying to be socially acceptable have only hamstrung us. Being labeled a hater by those who don't even understand what love is because they are too busy looking for ways to be offended does not concern me, because I am a barbarian in Christ and I know that my heart is right before my God. I don't *hate* anyone; quite the contrary, I love even those who hate me because that is one of the laws written on my heart—in fact, it is the primary law, and other than the admonition to "love the Lord my God with all my heart and all my soul and all my mind"— it is the only law I need to remember.

Everything I do must be motivated by one of two loves—loving God and loving my neighbor—and it is the passion that love engenders in my soul that drives me, that strengthens me, that gets me up in the morning, puts my feet on the path before me, and keeps me storming the gates as the enemy tries in vain, time and again, to steal away those I love and to discourage me.

I am a barbarian with a Bible and I will not be stopped. My heart is a house of prayer and zeal for my God consumes me! This barbarian is a *Jesus freak*; I am a freak in the eyes of the world because the Spirit of the living God within me drives me to be the best husband, father, friend, brother, son, and pastor—the best *person*—that I can be. I do that by passionately loving all the people in my life that the Lord has entrusted me with. By laying down my life for them.

I don't work for worldly gain and fame; I don't clamor for more stuff and I don't even really care if everyone likes me. I know who I am and I know whom I follow—the one who was not too well liked either. In fact, they killed him—they hated him so much—because he would not play their games; he would not listen to the experts and submit to the wise. But what he did, he did because of his great love, love that we could never fathom, a love that laid down everything for those he loved—you and me.

He didn't do that so that we could live our lives shackled to someone else's oars as slave in a ship that we are not even sure is going anywhere. The Viking barbarians rowed their own ships when they weren't under sail, as free men who all knew where they were going and why. There was no room for slaves. Slaves took up space that the fighting men and women needed, and rowing kept them strong—ready for the fight. The Greeks and the Romans—the *civilized*—used slaves to pull their oars, forcing people to go where they did not want to go to further their own agendas. There was no shared reward, no shared vision, and no passion, only weariness and dread. Sounds like some of our churches.

We, the church, are supposed to be free to choose which ship to join. Few Vikings ever got very far trying to set off by themselves. Can you imagine the lone Viking splashing ashore after jumping from his little dragon-headed canoe? "I am here to pillage. Lay down your arms and surrender your gold and your land!" No, they pulled together for a reason; strength in numbers, unity of purpose.

The Vikings only made it to Iceland, Greenland, and North America by pulling together as they sailed unknown waters that half a millennium later would scare the pants off the first Spanish explores as they were sure they were sailing off the edge of the world. There had to be a sense of unity, trust, and determination to make those voyages. It was the barbarian sense of purpose and the simplicity of that purpose—one they had all agreed upon—that got them through the ice-cold waves as they sought to build new lives for those they loved. And that is what drove them; the majority of the Viking conquests were made by men and women looking for better lives, for places where they could settle down in peace, farm and fish, raise children, and just live. Pretty simple—care for those you love.

Where is your ship going—and why?

CHAPTER 3

A BARBARIAN AFTER GOD'S OWN HEART

. . . a man after my own heart; he will do everything I want him to do. (Acts 13:22)

I WANT TO start this chapter with a quick overview; it's actually the first thing I wrote back when I was first pondering why I would even consider lifting up the barbarian as any sort of role model. A quick sketch, if you will, that laid the prayerful foundation of what this barbarian in the kingdom notion is all about. The following synopsis is the heart of this teaching and is where we are headed in the chapters to follow.

The barbarian is . . .

The barbarian in the kingdom is a man, a simple man with a simple mission: to live victoriously and to never be ashamed of the gospel of Jesus Christ. The barbarian in the kingdom makes no apologies for who he is as a man or as a soldier for Christ. The barbarian in the kingdom takes care of his own, especially the women in his life. Not because he believes they are inferior and weak, but because that is his role and he embraces it. The barbarian women in his life appreciate and thrive in the freedom and security that his care affords them.

It is the civilized and religious man who subjugates and diminishes his woman. In the barbarian tradition, as in the kingdom of God, the women always play a key and equal—even if different—role in the societal and family structure. They are not ashamed to be women and the men are not ashamed to be men. Barbarian men and women recognize that this gender neutralism business pervading our society today is just as ridiculous and absurd as was the notion that women are inferior.

The barbarian in the kingdom lives by a simple heart cry: "I desire to do your will, my God; your law is within my heart" (Ps. 40:8).

That's the simplicity of the barbarian nature guided by an instinct of justice uncluttered by burdensome religious rules or politically correct gamesmanship. This allows him or her to move freely and effectively, advancing and strengthening the kingdom while hardly even realizing it and moving in the three basic tenets that are ingrained in the soul of every person who is wise enough and courageous enough to embrace it—the tenets that reflect the Spirit and life of our Savior:

Simplicity of purpose. Singularity of mission. Determination of spirit.

And that's why we need barbarians in the kingdom.

To me, this synopsis of the barbarian mindset sounds a lot like a model for a healthy family and a healthy church as well. It is in fact the way I strive—and have to keep reminding myself—to lead the church family that I pastor.

The barbarian after God's own heart

So in this chapter I want to look at the barbarian *man* and what we can learn from him today, we men who strive to serve our families and our God.

What does it mean to be a man? The barbarian of old had little trouble with this notion; there was little confusion over what it meant to be a man in the barbarian tribes, wherever and whenever they were found. The barbarian man's measure was taken in large part by his strength—physical prowess—his courage and his ability to defend and provide for his family, his home, and his clan.

He was not ashamed to be a man nor was he discouraged from being a man—in all his testosterone-driven fury and glory. What a difference from where we are today where being a man is almost something we have to apologize for as traditional manly traits are being frowned upon. Our society has gone from being one of extreme manly narcissism that looked down on the female of the species as inferior and silly, to being one where the true man has to be stuffed down and hidden deep inside and forcibly trained to be sensitive and effeminate. "Yes dear, no dear, shall I hold your purse? Oh, look it matches my shoes; yes, I would love to hear about all the gossip you heard at the spa. Maybe next week we can go together and get a pedicure with matching polish—oh, the guys at work will be so jealous!"

Popular culture would make you believe that all women want men who are not just in touch with their feminine side, but live there most of the time, and that most men are stupid, bumbling, or egoistical idiots who need to be retrained and tolerated, softened and civilized. Interesting, you never see a pencil-necked geek wearing skinny jeans and wielding a smart phone on the cover of a romance novel—just saying.

Does the barbarian in the heart of all women really want a man to be just a woman with a deeper voice? I think when it comes down to it, a woman wants a man to be a man, a man wants a woman to be a woman, and that's a barbarian notion that's hard to shake, and I contend should not be shaken, in spite of what the world tells us. God made us very different both physically and psychologically. We have different physical makeups, our brains are wired differently, and we have different hormones that do everything from accentuate our physical differences to cause us to react very differently emotionally to pretty much everything.

But in our politically correct—"Let's make everyone the same so that everything is fair for everyone"—world, where it's how we feel about something that's important, rather than what is real and true, it is getting harder and harder to be a man. I see it constantly in the younger generation as this mindset is starting to have a real impact on young men—they are having an identity crisis. I see it at work in my construction job; I see it in the churches—everywhere, young men getting more and more frustrated, confused, and angry because they aren't allowed to be men.

Most of them don't have real men teaching them how to be a man—how to contain and direct the barbarian inside aching to be loosed—so they either act like immature idiots or they just become subjugated doormats, wondering why the woman they have bowed down to does not respect them. Women, whether they admit it or not, need heroes and leaders. And men need to be heroes and lead. This goes back to that love and respect thing we find spelled out in the Scriptures—a woman needs to feel loved and a man needs to feel respected. "Nevertheless let each one of you in particular so love his own wife as himself, and let the wife *see* that she respects *her* husband" (Eph. 5:33 NKJV).

Though I would love to delve more deeply into this concept of distinct family roles and the importance of loving and respecting in a marriage, I have done this in previous books so I won't belabor it here. My point is that the next generation is losing all understanding of this concept and they are floundering as a result.

Barbarian mentoring

We need barbarian mentoring. The barbarians in the kingdom need to rise up and take the next generation under their wings and show them what it means to be a man. We need to invite the young men to stand with us side by side in the shield wall. This sounds like a huge task—teaching manliness—but it's really not, unless of course you do not know what it means to be a man. Guys my age or older (baby boomers) have an advantage; we were raised by the generation of warriors that saved the world from Nazism and imperialist Japan.

We had fathers or grandfathers, uncles and bosses who fought in a world war, together as men with a single simple purpose: to save the world, including their own homes and families, from an enemy that they were allowed to call an enemy, to fight a fight that they were allowed to win and did win. And they returned home from the battlefields with that same spirit of accomplishment and pride and together build a better life for their families.

They were allowed and encouraged to work hard, and the harder they worked, the better off they were. These same men were raised during the Great Depression when there was no work so they relished the opportunity, the privilege of going to work and earning a dollar. They never took a paycheck for granted—nor anything else for that matter—they were men who raised sons to be men. Where did we lose that? I contend that we didn't; it just got tucked away as we got too comfortable living the fruits of what those men, and women, built for us. We just need to allow ourselves to once again be the men that our collective fathers and grandfathers were, God-fearing, hard-working, sacrificially loving men.

But just giving ourselves permission to be men is not enough. here is the key element: Men always need to affirm the next generation of men with time spent and words spoken. It's a curious thing that a boy will never feel like a man until someone who is a man in his eyes tells him he is a man, preferably their father. We no longer have rites of passage that mark the day when a boy becomes a man. We no longer expect anything of our young men and we no longer demand that they act like men. Personal responsibility and accountability have gone out the window and we have become an entitlement society. "I am entitled to a paycheck, I am entitled to health care, a smart phone, a car, an education, a place to live, internet—you name it, even if I didn't lift a finger to earn it."

On the other hand, we don't acknowledge hard work and responsibility like we should either—it just wouldn't be fair to everyone else. "Here's your participation trophy and a Pizza." We need to tell a young man when he has done the right thing, to acknowledge and affirm, "I sure appreciate the hard work you did, nice job." I always thank the guys who work on my jobs at the end of the day. If a guy knows you appreciate the effort he put into doing the job you asked him to do, he will come back the next day and work at it even more diligently. You have to give respect to get respect. Respect is the food that fuels the heart of the man. A *boy* looks for material gain and only takes; a *man* looks for and gives respect; and a man who is respected is able to love.

So what gets the boy across the line to manhood? Like I said, affirmation, that point in time when he was respected and affirmed as a man. Women won't understand this and that's fine, we'll talk about the barbarian woman in the next chapter, but right now trust me, ladies, that you also need to hear this for the sake of the men in your life. A man needs to *hear* these words or he will struggle with being a man for the rest of his life; here are the words—*I am proud of you*. And those words need to come from a father, or at least a father figure. It doesn't hurt to hear them from his wife either. You can take that to the bank. That is the respect pivot point between being a boy and becoming a man. Affirmation. Don't doubt me on this and don't poo poo it as silly.

Only a man who has been affirmed as a man can stop acting like a boy who is trying to get attention. Only a man who is comfortable in his manliness can be tender to his woman without seeming like a girly man. Only a man who is secure in his manliness can see the world through the eyes of his children without being immature and childish. Only a man who has been affirmed can rest at the end of a hard day without feeling like a loser or a poser. Only a man who has been affirmed can look in the mirror and like what he sees.

Ranch hand

In the West where reality is still a little more in your face than it is in a lot of places where big cities have replaced everything natural with manmade things and notions, we have a bit of an advantage on the man side of things. Especially on a ranch where if you don't take responsibility and work hard, things literally die. And there are things that need killing (like calf-killing coyotes and rabid skunks). It kind of keeps you grounded on the barbarian side of things; simplicity, tenaciousness, and common sense are requirements of survival in much of the west.

When I was ranching I often hired my nephews to come and help out—usually one or more of four nephews on Donna's side of the family who were not afraid to work, and I paid them generously, telling them, "If you do a man's work, you deserve a man's pay." I had them stacking hay, fencing, working cattle. We worked hard and I actually enjoyed teaching them how to work.

One of those nephews, Mike, who also lived next door, was one of my favorite victims . . . I mean, helpers. He was a big kid and I sometimes forgot how young he was as I worked him long and hard on hot summer days picking up and stacking hay, starting when he was twelve. One summer, I think he was sixteen or so, I told him I wanted him to start running the baler. So I showed him how to run the old Case tractor pulling the John Deere square baler, everything having to be just so to make a perfect bale with finicky equipment and not leave half the hay on the ground. He had it figured out in no time. Come time to pay him he was shocked to find out that I was giving him a couple of more dollars an hour.

I told him he was no longer an unskilled laborer so he was worth more money. The next week he wanted to argue again; he said he felt really guilty taking more money when it felt like he wasn't working as hard. I explained a little more clearly this time, "Mike, what you are doing takes more skill. It is something not everyone can do and it is a bigger responsibility. I am trusting you out there all alone on that tractor because I know you can get the job done. That makes you worth more money."

He told me a few years later that when I told him that, his whole perspective on work and the value of what he was worth changed. And he thanked me. I don't take credit for him becoming a man, his father had a much bigger hand in that than I did, but I think that was a pivotal moment for him. He was affirmed by someone he trusted and respected, he was affirmed as a man by another man—his uncle. And he is still one of the hardest-working responsible men you will ever meet.

Men need affirmation. But that's not enough either. We are, even after all that, still in need of a little—sometimes a lot—of tempering once the man in us is released. That's where God the Father comes in. The difference between a man who is simply a barbarian, and a *barbarian after God's own heart*, is that the barbarian in the kingdom has been affirmed by God. Only a barbarian who has been affirmed by God as a man can be a man after God's own heart—a barbarian after God's own heart.

David son of Jesse, the lowly shepherd boy become a king, would receive the greatest affirmation a man could ever receive. Hundreds of years after his death, the apostles Paul and Luke are still quoting God the Father as calling David "A man after my own heart." "After removing Saul, he made David their king. God testified concerning him: 'I have found David son of Jesse, a man after my own heart; he will do everything I want him to do" (Acts 13:22).

Now there's an affirmation. There's something to be remembered for.

David was a man who was anointed as the next king before he was old enough to grow a decent beard. Shortly after that, he killed the champion of the dreaded Philistines, a thirteen-foot-tall behemoth of a man named Goliath. He spent years living in exile as the leader of a band of rogues whose numbers reached to the point of being a sizable army. He was finally crowned king, captured the ancient stronghold called Jerusalem from the Jebusites who had lived there since a time long before anyone could remember, and turned it into the capital city of what would soon become one of the wealthiest and most influential kingdoms on earth, under the rule of David and then his son Solomon. And he would establish the throne and the lineage that the Messiah himself would spring from—and that's just the highlights.

Yet for all his accomplishments as a warrior king, he is remembered and referred to as "a man after God's own heart." A man with a heart for God who would write songs that touch the hearts of people still today. Songs that the church today sings every Sunday, usually without even realizing it. And the words of his heart of passion and simplicity of purpose still bring people, men and women, to their knees before the throne of God today.

David achieved what every man yearns to achieve: affirmation as a man from his Father, in this case, his Father God. He got to be the *hero* over and over, and he is remembered because he made a difference. He was thrown for a loop when his first love, and wife Michal disrespected him, mocking him for his "undignified" behavior, and I think this became cause for some of the more foolish things he did. But in the end he became the man he was created to be.

He made a difference because he was a man after God's own heart because he knew who he was and he *was* who he was. But because he had allowed God into the innermost places of his heart—a barbarian heart that loved the right and hated the wrong, that was determined and patient at the same time—he was able to write and speak words that poets and songwriters would try to emulate, and often just outright use, for millennia.

That's why David, a man with the spirit of a barbarian—who in moments of weakness could be ruthless and conniving to the point of astonishment to the more civilized sensibilities of today's readers of his story—could be called a man after God's own heart. To be honest with you, I still have a hard time reconciling all that David did with the "man after God's own heart" notion. He did some really bad things; murder, adultery, having multiple wives all at once, and he and his band of rogues even offered themselves as mercenaries to the enemies of the people he was anointed to rule. David surely had barbarian tendencies, many unfettered and undisciplined especially as a younger man—yet God loved him and trusted him, giving him chance after chance, honing the young barbarian into a true king, a man of God, and man's man. I may not understand it, but it surely gives me a lot of hope. God didn't crush the barbarian heart of David, he patiently strengthened and enhanced the positive while revealing to David the folly of some of his baser instincts.

David was a man with all the flaws of any man; in fact, he was an extreme man who lived his life to the max and when he fell he fell hard. But he was also a man who knew how to repent—when to turn and face his Father God. I wouldn't be surprised to learn that David was a manic depressive, a man capable of such extreme passion and emotion that he was often out of control. Yet when he turned his heart to God, knowing there was no other way out, he would put *all* his hope and trust in Him, and at that point he was invincible. He knew that without his God he was a train wreck (a chariot wreck?) looking for a place to happen. But with his God—nothing on this earth could stand in the way of his accomplishing what God had put on his heart.

God's not looking for perfect people; he is looking for people who are not afraid to throw themselves out there and be real, to be everything they know how to be, to attack life head on and not get hung up in self-doubt and excuses. When David fell he fell hard, but his next move would be to fall on his knees and cry out to his God from the very depths of his troubled soul and he would get back up stronger than ever. That's what a man does—that's a barbarian after God's own heart.

That's what a cowboy—the truest manifestation of the barbarian spirit we have today—does. When you fall off the horse you get right back on, you learn from it, figure out what went wrong, and you don't do it again because it hurts. Above all, you don't let the horse get the better of you or you will always fear the horse and the horse will never respect you.

David was a man who looked at his mistakes and resolved not to stay down. Hear the words of a barbarian after God's own heart as he comes to the Lord to beg forgiveness for arranging the death of the husband of the woman he has knocked up in an attempt to hide his immorality:

> For I know my transgressions, and my sin is always before me. Against you, you only, have I sinned and done what is evil in your sight; Hide your face from my sins and blot out all my iniquity.
>
> Create in me a pure heart, O God, and renew a steadfast spirit within me. Do not cast me from your presence or take your Holy Spirit from me. Restore to me the joy of your salvation and grant me a willing spirit, to sustain me . . .
>
> My sacrifice, O God, is a broken spirit; a broken and contrite heart you, God, will not despise. (Ps. 51:3–12, 17)

The man the Lord affirms is a man who is strong enough to admit when he is weak, a man who is strong enough to find his strength in God and keep pushing on with a renewed sense of determination of spirit, simplicity of purpose, and singularity of mission—the mission being to be the man God called him to be. That's the man who will be remembered; that's the man who can and will conquer anything that gets thrown in his way. And that's the man who will not just be part of the kingdom, but will *build* the kingdom.

A desire to do God's will

Remember what God said about David? He is "a man after my own heart; he will do everything I want him to do."

Does that bring anything to mind? How 'bout one of our barbarian key verses: "I desire to do your will, my God; your law is within my heart" (Ps. 40:8).

These words were also written by David. That is why David could be a man after God's own heart, because his singular mission and purpose—even though he had to constantly fight the flesh, which had its own singular mission to lead him astray—was to do God's will. Not out of religious duty, not to impress anyone, but because he loved his God. He loved his God because he knew his God could be trusted. His God was always there for him when he called, always faithful when it mattered, and everything his God did he did out his love for David and all who put their trust in him.

The same thing a real man does. A man can be trusted, is there when he is called on, and does everything he does out of a love for those who look to him. That's why the Lord led me to devote much of this writing to what it means to be a man, why we look to the barbarian to see what a man is supposed to be. Because a man with the simple *barbarian with a Bible* credo of desiring to do the will of God as is written on his heart—is a man after God's own heart. And that's all God wants: obedience with character and strength.

That's a man God can use. A man who will take care of those God loves, those God has entrusted to him—his wife and children, a man who will stand in the shield wall side by side with other men no matter the threat, no matter how dark, and no matter how hard. Because he *has to*. It is his nature. A real man *wants* to be a hero, he cherishes his woman, and he wants to take care of those he loves. It is his nature and it is a good thing. We have been robbed of that; let's take it back, or you will be just another forgotten face in the crowd.

A man also wants to be remembered, to leave a mark, to know that he mattered. There is only one sure way to do that: Be brave enough to live a life of passion, passion for life and passion for God. You may not have bards and poets writing and singing of your exploits, but you will be remembered by those who knew you and by your Father, as a man after God's own heart. And unlike forgotten poems and songs, that *is* forever. Stop making excuses and looking for things to blame for your failures—you are a man, and you have the Spirit of God, who conquered death itself! As my boss at the *Billings Livestock Commission* (a livestock auction yard) used to tell me when I worked there as a teenager, "Cowboy up!"

"The Lord is with me; I will not be afraid. What can mere mortals do to me? The Lord is with me; he is my helper. I look in triumph on my enemies" (Ps. 118:6–7).

The barbarian in the kingdom is a man who, as long as he is tuned in to God, can conquer anything.

No longer a boy

Speaking of my former boss at the Billings Livestock Commission, the summer I turned seventeen I decided I wanted to go to work at one of the public auction yards in town. I had been working at a clothing store after school, cleaning up and doing everything no one else wanted to do, and really wanted something more challenging. I went to the first yard, found the foreman out in the yard, and announced that I was looking for work. He looked down at me from atop his horse and asked, "How old are you?"

I replied, "Sixteen, almost seventeen."

He quickly dismissed me, declaring that I "was too young."

So undeterred and a little angry at being disrespected so, I drove out to the edge of town where there was another yard, found the foreman, Dan Monroe, in the yard house, and made the same declaration: "I'm looking for work, you need anybody?" He looked me up and down, asked if I had a saddle, and I said I could get one. He told me to go to the main office, fill out a job application, and be there at 7:00 on Thursday morning for sale day.

I worked my tail off that summer, chasing cows, feeding livestock, fixing fences, cleaning the sale ring (the arena where the animals are shown and bid on), stacking hay—I mean *semi-trailer loads* of hay. At the end of the summer I went to punch out for the day and Dan told me, "Why don't you come in Monday?" the implication being that he was going to make me full time. I looked at him kind of surprised and said, "I have to start school Monday."

He looked surprised so I said, "I'm a junior at *Billings Senior."* He looked at me rather incredulously and said, "I just figured anyone who could buck bales like you was out of school by now."

That was forty years ago now and I remember those words like it was last week. This will sound weird but, in my mind, at that moment I became a man. My whole sense of who I was changed. I had ridden high-strung cowponies with real cowboys, stacked semi loads of hay by hand under a blazing Montana sun, been charged at and kicked by half-crazed cows, busted holes through concrete with a spud bar and a sledge hammer in order to replace broken fence posts—I worked with such relish that I had earned the name "Wild Man" from the cowboys I sweated alongside of—and now I had to go back to school and sit in a classroom like a little kid.

But I was no longer a kid, I was a man—*Wild Man.* I had been declared a man by the men I worked with and more importantly, by 'Ol Dan Monroe, former rodeo champion and now auction yards foreman—my boss. My whole perspective had changed. I was confident and knew that I could do whatever I set my mind to. It no longer mattered what others thought of me; I knew who I was and I liked who I was.

Who is looking for you to affirm them? Be that man, it just takes a word.

CHAPTER 4

The BARBARIAN WOMAN

Love . . . bears all things, believes all things, hopes all things, endures all things. (1 Cor. 13:4–7 NKJV)

IN THIS CHAPTER I am going to, with fear and trembling, tackle the really big subject of *the barbarian woman*. Having been married to one (my Norwegian wife) and raised by one (my Swedish/Irish/English mother)—and having raised three barbarian daughters, I have made a few observations—things necessary for survival, my survival.

As you know, I have contended that the barbarian approach is more of a state of mind than it is a genetic disposition, but when you are directly descended from those for whom the term *barbarian* was first coined—those unconquered peoples living in the northern forests of Europe—you are, perhaps, a little more predisposed to barbarian ways.

When Donna and I got engaged she was worried about telling her Norwegian (and proud) grandmother that she was marrying a Swede. With a name like *Swaningson* it was pretty hard to conceal. My grandfather, Anders Svenningsson, migrated here from Sweden and later Americanized his name (thank you!). Why the Swedes and Norwegians have had this animosity towards each other is still somewhat of a mystery to me, but it didn't matter. When you make a barbarian mad, they are mad for a very long time—especially the women. As the old Swedes like to say, "You can always tell a Norwegian, but you can't tell them much!"

I joke with my girls that if they feel an inner turmoil sometimes it is because the Swede and Norwegian within them are fighting each other. And no, you don't want to cross them—not only did they inherit the heart of their barbarian ancestors but I raised them to be strong and to take care of themselves, to demand and expect respect and to be treated like a lady. They can skin a buck and change a flat tire but they shouldn't have to if there is a man around who knows his place. A barbarian woman knows how to let the barbarian man be the hero he desires to be and is strong enough to *not* allow herself to be bullied or to find herself without recourse.

A couple of years ago I got a call from my daughter Jessie; she was at a convenience store buying oil for her car and wanted to add it but couldn't get the oil lid off on her engine. I told her to try and find a rag and use it to grab ahold of the cap for a better grip. I then said if that doesn't work find a guy that doesn't look scary and ask him to help you. Most any decent guy will jump at the chance to help a damsel in distress. It's our nature to want to help the ladies; it's what a gentleman does. Society is trying its best to wipe out that chivalrous code but it is still deeply ingrained in the heart of the barbarian that lurks within us all. Sure enough, she soon had a helpful young man cheerfully helping her get the stubborn lid off and he even offered to put the oil in for her.

You see, there's a give and take there. I have tried to teach my girls to be strong and independent but at the same time to allow the male of the species room to be the gentleman, to do the dirty stuff they are good at if they are in a place where that can be done safely. That's one of the things I have always admired about their mother; she's not a girly girl who can't do anything for herself but greatly appreciates it if I do the things for her that I might be better at. I am very proud of all my daughters. They are all strong-willed and courageous in their own unique ways. Sometimes they learned things the hard way, and sometimes they actually listened to their barbarian parents. They have become women of real character with amazing work ethics, strength of character, and naturally loving hearts that have been shaped and strengthened by their love for their Savior and his love for them.

The heart of the barbarian within a woman, however, can cause real trouble, just as it can in men, unless we learn how to harness it, using its strength to magnify the Lord in us while tempering the flesh which, left unchecked, can consume us. So let's explore this woman barbarian notion some; just how do we manage these wild women?

A little background first.

Hearth and home

In the barbarian tribes of old, whether it be the Celts, the Brits, the Franks, Goths, Germans, or Norse, etc., the woman always played a vital role in society. Women were not considered to be inferior except in physical strength and sometimes that was even debatable. There are notable examples in Celtic and Norse histories and sagas of women leading men in battle as raiders and defenders. The men had no qualms about following a strong woman who had proven her mettle in battle and proffered sound strategies. The even-keeled stoicism and courage of the barbarian woman were very conducive to leading warriors on the field of battle.

But for the most part, barbarian women found their satisfaction as the keepers of the home and hearth, overseeing the business of making the house a home; keeping their kids and their men in line. They did this while enjoying a measure of protection found in the superior strength of their men, coupled with the knowledge that the barbarian women could also defend what was theirs against whatever enemy (if need be) herself. You don't mess with bear cubs *or* the children of the barbarian woman—the results will be about the same.

Oftentimes this was of necessity as the men would be off hunting, fishing, or raiding, leaving the women largely alone to be the overseers and defenders of the homes, families, and villages. Not only were the women capable but they proved time and again that they were not to be trifled with, especially when it came to defending their children or their honor. The mighty Viking warrior and explorer may have ruled the seas but at home he was just *Sven,* the man with the barbarian appetite, who made messes and brought home fish, and foul-smelling britches that needed to be washed.

If he *didn't* bring home the fish or treat his woman right, he might just find himself out in the cold; Viking women were actually allowed to divorce their husbands, if they felt they were being mistreated or not adequately provided for or protected. But for the most part, a mutual respect and love in the barbarian home—a condition that was essential simply to survive in the natural and often unfriendly world—prevailed.

The barbarian family needed a strong woman who was grounded in reality and not afraid to face the world with her head held high while being supportive of her man with whom she reared strong, confidant children, children who were prepared to face the world knowing they were loved because they saw love lived out before and for them, in their mother. The barbarian woman exudes confidence, and this is a beauty that cannot be outshone. This confidence—not worrying about pleasing everyone, measuring up, or whether others find her attractive—frees her to love, to give, and to recognize her blessings.

In the first chapter of Luke we find a woman who recognized her blessings and clung tenaciously to what was important: her faith, her husband, and the promises that brought her hope and did not disappoint.

Elizabeth

The Lord showed me the heart of the barbarian woman in what seemed to be a very unlikely place, the story of Elizabeth, the wife of a priest named Zechariah. Elizabeth was a woman who deeply loved her husband and her God, who never gave up hope despite appearances, and didn't desire anything of life but that she could be a wife and a mother, to have and to hold a family of her own.

Elizabeth was also a descendant of Aaron. Both of them were righteous in the sight of God, observing all the Lord's commands and decrees blamelessly. But they were childless because Elizabeth was not able to conceive, and they were both very old. . . .

> "Then an angel of the Lord appeared to him, standing at the right side of the altar of incense. When Zechariah saw him, he was startled and was gripped with fear. But the angel said to him: 'Do not be afraid, Zechariah; your prayer has been heard. Your wife Elizabeth will bear you a son, and you are to call him John'" (Luke 1:11-13).

John and Elizabeth had faith and determination that got the attention of their Lord. You can bet that Elizabeth had prayed daily her entire adult life for a child, and now the Lord had answered her passionate prayers, prayers that she had surely been tempted to give up on ever being heard as the years passed. But she knew the stories of Sarah and Hannah; her God was a God of miracles.

So when her husband came home and finally managed to communicate to her what had happened—that he had seen an angel of the Lord in the temple who had promised him that God would indeed bless them with a son—her hope blazed anew. Her faith, held passionately and securely within her heart, rejoiced and she accepted the promise from the Lord even when her husband's faith had wavered, leaving Zechariah mute for the duration of his wife's pregnancy. "Blessed is she who has believed that the Lord would fulfill his promises to her!" (Luke 1:45).

She didn't worry about whether or not she was worthy. No doubt she had heard for years, "There must be sin in your life or else God would not have shut your womb!" She was righteous in the sight of God; *blameless*, still, she had no children—yet. Who knows why they didn't have children, but we know it wasn't a punishment, you need to hear that. Sometimes things just happen; it doesn't mean you are bad or your faith is too weak. Elizabeth trusted God's goodness and God noticed this, the quiet resolve of this humble woman who didn't blame God or herself for her desires not being granted, and decided she was just the one he needed to raise a barbarian prophet named John—it was time to grant her the desire of her heart.

God chose a woman with a heart of simple purpose, who had a spirit determined to fulfill her singular mission—to raise the prophet who would proclaim the coming of the Lord: John the Baptist. The radical prophet who would live in the desert shunning all the comforts and trappings of the civilized and religious, eating locusts and wild honey and wearing camels' hair robes; an Israelite living like a barbarian, proclaiming the coming of the Messiah who would open the gates of heaven to everyone—even to the barbarian Gentiles. I think only a woman with the heart of a barbarian could raise a man like that. A heart that loves fully because it is uncluttered with the unnecessary and meaningless, unburdened with lies and condemnation. Let's read some more of the story from Luke: When it was time for Elizabeth to have her baby, she gave birth to a son. Her neighbors and relatives heard that the Lord had shown her great mercy, and they shared her joy.

On the eighth day they came to circumcise the child, and they were going to name him after his father Zechariah, but his mother spoke up and said, "No! He is to be called John."

When it was time for Elizabeth to have her baby, she gave birth to a son. Her neighbors and relatives heard that the Lord had shown her great mercy, and they shared her joy.

On the eighth day they came to circumcise the child, and they were going to name him after his father Zechariah, but his mother spoke up and said, "No! He is to be called John."

They said to her, "There is no one among your relatives who has that name."

Then they made signs to his father, to find out what he would like to name the child. He asked for a writing tablet, and to everyone's astonishment he wrote, "His name is John." Immediately his mouth was opened and his tongue set free, and he began to speak, praising God. (Luke 1:57-64)

I love this part of the story. I can just picture all the grey beards and sanctimonious busybodies gathered for the ritual of circumcision and the all-important official naming of the first and only son. I can just hear the family of Zechariah proudly and solemnly proclaiming him to be *Zechariah Ben Zechariah*, thinking they are honoring the old man and doing him a favor in making the proclamation since he has been rendered mute ever since that day in the temple nine months earlier.

But Elizabeth speaks up and says, "No! His name is John." Imagine the looks that went around the room "Who does this woman think she is?" Women in this culture did not tell men what to do, certainly not in religious matters or the all-important family name to which their whole heritage was tied both spiritually and materially. Israelites took their names very seriously. They spoke not just of their identity but also tracked their past and determined their future—their forever.

But Elizabeth was not to be cowed. She knew what God had planned for her and tradition and protocol be darned. Interesting that God chose not to loosen old Zach's tongue until the moment that he confirmed his wife; both the Lord *and* Zechariah came to her defense "Listen to her, she knows a thing or two." Because she had the courage of her conviction to speak out what she knew to be right—because of the barbarian heart of Elizabeth—God's purpose was accomplished.

Imagine if she had given up, just toed the mark, kept her head down, and embraced the pressure of a thousand years of her male-dominated culture and tradition silencing her and browbeating her into passivity, or the condemnation that must have been all around her as a childless old woman. Picture the looks in the marketplace, the condescending remarks in the synagogue, but she kept her head up, kept moving forward, always knowing that tomorrow was another day to live and love and hold on to hope. And her hope was not disappointed.

So what motivates the heart of a barbarian woman in the kingdom? *Love.*

> Love is patient, love is kind. It does not envy, it does not boast, it is not proud. It does not dishonor others, it is not self-seeking, it is not easily angered, it keeps no record of wrongs. Love does not delight in evil but rejoices with the truth. It always protects, always trusts, always hopes, always perseveres. (1 Cor. 13:4-7)

To me, this verse says everything you need to know about the barbarian woman in the kingdom. She is love personified, not the mushy "everything is sunshine and roses" fragile kind of love that can be shaken to the core at the first sign of trouble, but the passionate deep down ingrained love that can overcome anything the world or the enemy throws at her. A love that can bear all things and come out stronger in the end. A love that is patient and rational when all others around her are lost in emotional chaos or jealous pettiness.

She does not rejoice in the hurt of others but is strong enough to allow even those she loves to experience the consequences of their own foolishness should they refuse to listen to her warnings. And she will be there to pick them up when they land in the mud face first, with a firm hand and a gentle smile offering another chance to choose the right.

The barbarian woman is not given to hysteria or panic. Her emotions, though deeply felt, are not on the surface causing her to lose control.

If she does, you had better run for the hills, but for the most part she is in control. This allows her to think through, to listen and observe, seeking truth and resolution before running or attacking. The fight or flight mechanism prevalent in the man is controlled in the woman by an instinct to protect and nurture. She knows that she can best serve her family by remaining calm, and she often has to be the eyes and ears of her barbarian man to direct his sometimes-misguided fury. She is the radar he needs to hit the mark without destroying the village. I'll let you figure that one out . . .

A woman hears and understands things—call it a spiritual discernment or woman's intuition—that men sometimes blissfully miss. The danger in this is that women can also be offended a little too easily and hold grudges way too long. They are very tuned in to the perceptions of others, particularly what others think of them.

Self-worth

This brings me to a very important point. The key reason we need to adopt the barbarian mindset is to engender emotionally healthy women in the kingdom of God, women who are able to accept the love of a Father God who loves them for who they are. If you want to be a woman who is able to be strong and courageous, even-keeled—even stoic when need be, while at the same time loving passionately and unselfishly—you cannot, and must not, allow your sense of self-worth to be determined by what others think of you. This is the biggest pit that women fall into, starting as little girls. The very first time a little girl comes home from school—probably kindergarten—crying, it's because another little girl did not like her, told her that her dress was ugly, her hair was ugly, she was stupid, or she didn't want to be her friend anymore . . . she starts the descent into that pit of self-doubt.

Little boys will laugh insults off or punch each other and move on, but a little girl will hold on to this hurt for a good long time, and it will build—snowball—as the years go by. Cliques are formed, the peer groups of the cool girls, the sleepovers you were excluded from, never being able to wear the right clothes or the right shoes. Middle school is a living nightmare and high school is just something to bear as your loser status is now engraved in stone. Or if you are one of the *chosen ones*, the cool kids, you get out of your "everybody worships me" world and discover that you really don't have the world by the tail and no one cares who you hung out with in school.

The little girl who was convinced by others that she was either a loser or a princess is now totally without an identity. She doesn't know who she is and will never be happy, never be satisfied with the person she sees in the mirror. This leads to all sorts of disastrous ends: eating disorders, drug addictions, depression, promiscuity—even suicide.

Ladies, mothers *and* fathers, this is something you both need to work on; your daughters need barbarian mentoring just as much as young men do and it has to start as soon as they become self-aware. As soon as they hear the words, "What a beautiful little girl," and know what it means, they have to be taught that who they are, their worth, is not tied up in their looks, their style, who likes them, and who doesn't. They have to know that their worth is not tied to what others think about them.

Barbarians *do not* connect their self-worth to what others think of them. They do not care if everyone does not like them. Barbarians know what is inside of them, what is in their hearts, because they have been taught what is right and wrong. It is *written on their hearts* and the person laughing at you, calling you stupid and ugly, does not, *cannot*, know what is in your heart—only you can. With the exception of one other Person, Jesus.

> "For it was you who formed my inward parts; you knit me together in my mother's womb. I praise you because I am fearfully and wonderfully made; your works are wonderful, I know that full well" (Ps. 139:13–14).

He created your heart, he made you who you are for a reason, and he loves you. He created you to love and to live with a passion that is a reflection of him, that is driven by the ability to love with a determination and a fierceness that can burn through any darkness anyone would try to throw at you. You are perfect because God *made* you that way, and whatever you messed up along the way . . . he has redeemed—so you are still perfect! "For by one sacrifice he has made perfect forever those who are being made holy."

The Holy Spirit also testifies to us about this. First he says:

"This is the covenant I will make with them after that time, says the Lord. I will put my laws in their hearts, and I will write them on their minds" (Heb. 10:14–16).

Your strength, your value as a person, your worthiness to be loved, to be honored—to *be*—is found within, *deep* within, your heart where the Spirit of Jesus dwells and flourishes. If you are a barbarian woman in the kingdom, you belong to Jesus and you have the power of Christ, coupled with an innate sense of confidence that makes you dangerous—dangerous to the enemy who would try to mess with you or yours.

Confidence

Confidence: *That's* the thing that sets the barbarian woman apart. The barbarian woman in the kingdom of God—who has not succumbed to the unnaturally civilizing notions of taming the barbarian with religious expectations that only serve to leave her feeling like a failure, who has held on tenaciously to the spark of confidence and strength that God has planted in her soul and accepted the love of her Father through Jesus Christ—is a woman of confidence. She knows that her worth does not come from what others think of her. She knows that she is able, that she can do whatever she sets her mind to, that nothing can stand in her way—unless she allows it to. In any situation, in any place, she has an inner peace and calm because she knows that she is a precious soul, that she is loved, first and foremost by her Father God. And that is a love that can never be taken away or lost; it is a love that will never end.

So how do you get a woman to that barbarian notion of confidence, of liking herself? It took a lot of prayer and pondering as a man trying to figure out what I don't think most women even understand about themselves, but I think I finally put my finger on it. Just like a guy needs to hear from his father that he is proud of him, that he is a man, a girl needs to know that she is beautiful, and I don't mean just on the outside but also on the inside. We don't want girls to base their image of themselves on what others think of them, but we want them to know that they are beautiful.

For the young woman, the two are intricately intertwined. If she thinks she looks good, she will feel good. But you know what? Listen to this: If a woman *thinks* she looks good, she *will* look good—seriously— there is nothing more beautiful than a woman who is confident. It puts a spark in her eyes, which truly are the window to the soul. If the soul is healthy and beautiful, it will emanate from the eyes and light up the whole face. The posture will be better, the smile will take up residence on the face, and the love that engenders love will shine through.

I tease my daughter Jessie once in a while, "Everybody loves you!" It's true; if you know Jessie, you like her almost right away—why? Because she is a raving beauty? She is beautiful but so are a lot of women who not very likable. They like her because she is always smiling, her big hazel eyes sparkle and she just puts out the sense that she is always joyful, and people are drawn to that. That's confidence.

So how do we get our young barbarians there, to that beautiful confident place? I have always wondered when I tell a little girl—and we have several very pretty little girls in our church—"What a pretty dress you have on today, I love the braids in your hair" if I am doing them a disservice. Am I not teaching them that their worth is tied to their looks? But I think I might have figured it out, actually I think the Lord opened my eyes; it's okay for little girls to hear how pretty they are, as long as they are *also* hearing it from the ones in their lives who matter—their parents. The people they love and trust, who know them better than anyone else does, theirs is the opinion they need to hear.

Barbarian mothers, you need to continually reaffirm that your little girls are beautiful, and the mother's role differs a little from the father's. You need to teach them and model for them that their beauty isn't dependent on what they wear, how much makeup they put on, or how much skin they show. Your girls need you to teach them how to be beautiful, inside and out. If the world teaches them you will not like the results, I can guarantee you that.

> "Your beauty should not come from outward adornment, such as elaborate hairstyles and the wearing of gold jewelry or fine clothes. Rather, it should be that of your inner self, the unfading beauty of a gentle and quiet spirit, which is of great worth in God's sight" (1 Peter 3:3–4).

Fathers, here's your part: You need to *tell* your girls, including your wife, that they are beautiful, even if they act like they are embarrassed or they don't believe you. They need to hear it from you and here's why: If they do not hear it from you, dads, they will be constantly trying to hear it from someone else, and it will never be enough. I don't fully understand this, but it's true. A young woman who does not have her father's approval and love, expressed verbally—a woman needs words, she doesn't speak grunt like men do—will be forever trying to measure up and will never be happy with what she sees in the mirror. She will never have confidence and will never feel fully loved.

More beautiful

All who know my oldest daughter, Cally, would probably agree that she is confident. She has been tackling the world head on since the day she graduated from high school, and before. I remember the day this whole concept of telling the girls they are beautiful really hit home with me. We were hunting near Silesia, Montana, driving along from one place to another. Donna was in the front of the pickup and Cally was in the back seat; she was probably sixteen at this time. She was leaning forward to hear us and I turned around to look at her, all decked out in her finest blaze orange clothes, and for some reason it just struck me that she was really becoming a beautiful young lady. I looked again, and then again, deciding to use the opportunity to bless her.

She leaned back in the seat and said, "What!"

I said, "Every time I look at you, you get more beautiful!"

I can't really explain what happened at that moment but I sensed in my spirit that it was big. She didn't say a word but I could tell by the look on her face that something happened right then. I think this may have been one of those pivot points between self-doubt and self-confidence. I decided right then and there that I needed to make sure all of my daughters know how beautiful they are. I even resolved to write them a letter telling them so. This letter would become my first book, *To My Girls*, so that their *Heavenly Father* could tell all his girls they are beautiful and loved.

So tell the women and the little girls in your life: "You are truly beautiful." And make sure they really hear you. All of God's daughters are beautiful—including you, the barbarian mothers and daughters reading this.

"You are altogether beautiful, my darling; there is no flaw in you" (Song of Songs 4:7).

In a nutshell

I want to close this chapter with a little blurb I wrote as I was pondering the barbarian woman, a synopsis—to use the word I used in the previous chapter—of what a barbarian woman in the kingdom is.

The barbarian woman

The barbarian woman shares the passions of the barbarian man—she feels and fuels them longer and deeper than her male counterpart and fights to defend her own in her own way. She loves deeper, laughs louder, burns fiercer, and is unconcerned with the pettiness of the civilized. She is comfortable in her own skin and does not measure her worth by what you think of her or by how expensive her wardrobe or accessories are. She loves her man, her children, and her God and speaks her mind.

She says what she means, means what she says, and doesn't say anything just to be mean. If she lays you out with her words, then you needed it. Like the barbarian man, she prefers her life to be uncomplicated and uncluttered. Her weapons are her even-tempered determination, unshakable sense of what is right and true, and a steely-eyed look that will put the fear into the heart of any who would get in her way.

The barbarian woman perseveres through times of hardship and trial. Her resolve is strengthened by challenges. She faces them head-on and *always*—holds on to hope because she knows the sun will always come up tomorrow and she will have another chance to live, laugh, and love, without shame and without apology.

"Not only so, but we also glory in our sufferings, because we know that suffering produces perseverance; perseverance, character; and character, hope. And hope does not put us to shame, because God's love has been poured out into our hearts through the Holy Spirit, who has been given to us" (Rom. 5:3–5).

The barbarian woman loves fiercely and engenders a fierce love in return, a love that overcomes all things.

That's why we need barbarian women in the kingdom.

CHAPTER 5

ChE BARBARiaN'S STRENGTH

It is God who arms me with strength and keeps my way secure.
(2 Sam. 22:33)

THE BARBARIAN IN popular imagination and in history is characterized by strength. Look at the image we have in Conan—the ultimate barbarian portrayed in the original stories, the myriad of knock off stories, and the cheesy movies. I'm still trying to shake the 1980s image of Arnold Schwarzenegger as Conan from my mind. He had the physique but the rest just somehow didn't work for me, maybe it was the hair. But anyway, the barbarian is usually thought of as a strong person and we have talked about that—the physical strength, strength of character, strong-willed and determined, able and willing to stand against any enemy, and able to survive even the harshest environs and times.

We think of the Vikings, the terror from the north, tall and muscular, dwarfing most of their enemies and victims by their sheer size. There's the strong-willed and hardened northern Celts of the British Islands whom the Romans finally gave up on trying to conquer and literally built a wall—Hadrian's Wall—across the neck of northern Britain to keep at bay the wild-eyed and untamable blue-tattooed highlanders of what would later become Scotland and Ireland.

There are the savage Saxons, who would overrun the Brits after the Romans pulled out of Britain altogether, who would themselves be overrun by the Danes who would be ousted by the Saxons again, only to be subjugated by the Franks, all of whom would be overrun by the Normans . . . or something like that. The British Isles have been fought over by so many barbarian tribes that it's hard to keep track.

The Romans finally gave up and left because they had to be recalled to defend their own cities closer to home, as the barbarian Goths and Visigoths were pressing at the walls of Rome itself, while the Germans and the Huns were attacking its frontiers. I could go on and on; if you know world history at all, you know it has always been the strong, the fearless—overwhelming the comfortable and timid—who ruled the day.

The barbarian appetite for lands, power, and adventure is insatiable and left unchecked can be a terrible thing—certainly nothing to be proud of. But this makes it all the more amazing that the grace and power of God was sufficient and available to open the doors of the kingdom of heaven even to the barbarian. It has only been the ultimate infusion of the Word of God, enlivened by the Spirit of God, that has brought any modicum of peace and stability to the world.

I want to look back briefly at that man after God's own heart. Long before those barbarian hordes were infused into the kingdom by the blood of Jesus Christ, there was the strong man named David, a man of the land, a shepherd, exile, warrior, and King. In him we have a prime example of the barbarian mindset.

David, a man who certainly exhibited the qualities—both the good and the bad—of the barbarian, was a man of strength and resource. He may have been short in stature but he would prove to be a force to be reckoned with even by those who towered over him, including Goliath and King Saul. David survived trial after trial, even living as an exile in caves for several years of his life as he eluded King Saul, who would have killed him on sight and had attempted to do so numerous times in fits of jealous rage stemming from David's slaying of the giant Philistine Goliath.

David was certainly a man of great strength but he knew from where his true strength came, which is why he would be called a man after God's own heart even though his barbarian appetites and lusts sometimes got the best of him. There is a psalm of David recorded in 2 Samuel that leaves no doubt as to where David drew his strength from.

> As for God, his way is perfect: The Lord's word is flawless; he shields all who take refuge in him. For who is God besides the Lord? And who is the Rock except our God? It is God who arms me with strength and keeps my way secure. He makes my feet like the feet of a deer; he causes me to stand on the heights. He trains my hands for battle; my arms can bend a bow of bronze. You make your saving help my shield; your help has made me great. You provide a broad path for my feet, so that my ankles do not give way. (2 Sam. 22:31–37)

David could only do all that he did by finding his strength in the source of all strength, the strength that gave him the courage to put his physical, emotional, and leadership strengths to the test over and over again. It was only his faith in God that gave him the courage to face not just one giant, but several others, as he warred against the Philistines, to face men and armies from whom men much bigger and fiercer had run and hidden in terror. David never took credit for his own victories and never worried about the outcome of any battle so long as he trusted the Lord—desired and trusted that *his* will would be done. Even if he died in battle, if it was a battle the Lord chose for him, all would be well. In that he had a peace that could overcome anything. David found peace In the Lord's strength, in knowing that his heart was secure in his God.

We all need that. We need the strength of the Lord to find our peace. Our hearts will never have rest, will never find solace, will never be satisfied until we find our strength in the Lord—and in Him, our peace. This is critical for the barbarian because the one thing all barbarians share is a strong appetite, an appetite that can blind us and bind us, leaving a wake of destruction behind us as we seek more.

Go big

The barbarian with a Bible must find his strength, the strength that matters, in the Lord. This is the only way that we can keep the passions, the appetites—all the things that drive the barbarian in his simplicity and straightforward thinking—from consuming us. Barbarians always go big: big appetites—we love Thanksgiving, any reason to feast—big adventures, big spenders, big tires on big trucks. "Go big or go home, girly man!" If the barbarian finds something he likes, he can't get enough of it.

I discovered this about myself early on; I call it an addictive personality. When I like something, I want more—*more, more, more!* This is not good when you are talking about drugs or alcohol especially. There was a time when I had to drink the most, smoke the most, party the most, and indeed it took a miracle to free me from those addictions. But I have also been that way with other things: fishing, rappelling, hunting, hiking in the mountains . . . once I discovered something new and exciting, I couldn't get enough. This wasn't necessarily bad but it kind of worried me in my early days of walking with the Lord because when I was set free from the destructive addictions to drugs and drink by the overwhelming love of Jesus, I couldn't get enough of him. I devoured the Bible, I went to church two or three times a week and took part in every church-sponsored event or program I could.

I went a little overboard. I was indeed a barbarian new to the kingdom and I was going to pillage every nook and cranny of it and get everything I could out of it and gather as many as I could into my ship to help me conquer more. This wasn't necessarily bad either. What worried me was that I was afraid I was going to get tired of Jesus and lose interest. Like I said, I knew how I was, "Gimmee, gimmee, more, more, more." Okay I'm so over that. I've squeezed every ounce of fun out of that one, so let's move on. I feared this for many years, wondering when I was going to overdose on Jesus, wake up and realize that it wasn't doing it for me anymore, and just move on—or fall back.

It's been over thirty years now since I got zapped by the Holy Spirit and caught fire for Jesus and guess what? I haven't gotten tired of him yet, because *he is my strength* and without him, nothing else has any real meaning or value. Nothing can satisfy me or bring peace to my soul apart from Jesus. I cannot hold on to anything good without the strength of Jesus and I cannot avoid succumbing to everything bad without the strength of Jesus. He alone has satisfied my soul.

However, I *have* gotten tired of a lot of the church stuff as I got to the point where I became totally saturated with everything churchy, losing focus on what was truly important, losing that simplicity of purpose the barbarian is supposed to exemplify, getting caught up in the games of organized religion, and taking part in too many what I call "bless me" programs, either as the leader or the consumer. The consumer shows up, looks at the leader, and says, "Here I am, how can you bless me today?"

People expect way too much of leaders, who may be expecting way too much of themselves as they try to emulate or recreate a powerful move the Holy Spirit may have orchestrated at some point through them. "Well, it worked before, surely it will work again." That's how rituals are born, and rituals are religion, and religion is of man.

As soon as we think we have it figured out or that we are amazing ministers, teachers, worship leaders, dramatic arts people—whatever—we stop depending on or allowing the Lord to do the amazing part and we become just another poser—a false prophet or an entertainer. We must find, and keep finding, our strength in the Lord—or we will end up face down in a bowl of gruel. Speaking of the cheesy Arnold Schwarzenegger, *Conan the Barbarian,* the one scene that keeps coming back to me from that movie (maybe because I have so often felt this way) is when Conan has somehow come into some money so he ends up in this little trading post/village where there are all sorts of exotic enticements.

The young barbarian has never seen anything like this before and he goes hog wild, sampling everything to his heart's content. After a couple of days of nonstop partying, he is sitting down to have a bowl of gruel (or something) and he passes out from exhaustion and drunkenness, face first into his bowl. Fortunately, his friend sitting next to him grabs him by the hair and pulls him out of his soup before he drowns.

I have felt like that, partying all night, brooding at sunrise because the party is coming to an end, and I am still not satisfied. The thrill I thought I would achieve eluding me once again, the girl I was crushing on going home with someone else, the emptiness overwhelming as I face another day, hung over, broke, and alone. Just another barbarian trying to force a good time—to find satisfaction. "From the days of John the Baptist until now the kingdom of heaven has suffered violence, and men of violence take it by force" (Matt. 11:12 NKJV).

But I have felt like that in the church also, trying to force satisfaction into my soul; working, working, working to advance the kingdom through the church. Expending all my time and energy in whatever I was involved in—vacation Bible schools, camps, worship seminars, marriage seminars, Bible studies, classes; fixing, building, and maintaining church buildings—till I felt shell shocked and exhausted, ready to pass out in my soup. I was trying to take the kingdom by force—force of will and action that amounted to violence against my own sanity—climbing the church ladder to success, a success measured by recognition, position, salary, an office, and a following.

I kept throwing myself out there just *hoping* that it would finally get me to the place where someone would come along and say, "Okay, now it's time to do what you are supposed to be doing and here it is, here's your fulfillment." I thought my ultimate reward would be permission and release to do what I believed I was truly gifted and called by the Spirit of God to do, that someone important would recognize my potential. The worst part is, I really thought someone else—those I was told to submit to—would hear from the Lord what it was I was supposed to be doing and where.

Be the hunter

It doesn't happen that way. You cannot earn your satisfaction and no one is going to hand it to you, let alone tell you specifically where to find it. The soul-satisfying direction and purpose that God has specifically for you can come only from God. Peace can come only from God, peace in purpose and peace of mind. You can't go to enough programs and seminars to attain a higher spirituality, let alone a real peace. It is something that happens between you and God through Jesus by his Holy Spirit. It can happen in the midst of a crowd, but only because God managed to break through the noise and distractions enough to get your attention. "Here I am, walk with me." "Stop running in circles like you are trying to herd cats and become the hunter—quietly pursuing me with your eyes open, your ears tuned to the slightest sound of my voice, and your nose smelling the change of the winds and seasons as I move silently through the woods."

Determination of purpose and a singularity of mission—that's the barbarian following his own heart led by the Spirit of God. That's the successful hunter, that's a strong spirit that will find satisfaction and peace. Living for the pleasures of the flesh or working to build our fortunes: More stuff, bigger houses, newer cars, "faster horses, older whiskey, younger women, and more money" as the old song says, will leave you empty, even more so than when you had nothing. When you have what you thought you wanted, and you are still empty, it is a despair worse than death.

We know the world will leave us high and dry but living to work yourself to a frazzle for the church, or to consume all that the church can pump out for you (the two usually go hand in hand) will not get you satisfaction either. If we are seeking our strength, satisfaction, and fulfillment in the wrong places, we will be left standing on a hoard of tainted gold that we left a trail of broken bodies behind to acquire. And we will be more alone than ever before.

This radical church pillaging is dangerous, not just to those we shoved aside in the process—our families, friends, and whoever we deemed unworthy or were unwilling to man an oar in our longships—but to our own souls. Because once we have shaken the church down for all it's worth and we still are not satisfied and still do not have peace—we will turn back to the lusts of the flesh. Just like a dog returns to its vomit (see Prov. 26:11), the unsatisfied barbarian heart returns to its lusts.

"And the final condition of that person is worse than the first. That is how it will be with this wicked generation" (Matt. 12:45b).

It doesn't have to be this way. When I got to the point where I realized I wasn't on a ladder but on a treadmill, running for all I was worth but not getting anywhere but tired, God broke through to me, slowed me down long enough to get my attention to remind me from where my strength comes before I turned away from both the church and him altogether, as I have seen way too many barbarian warriors for Jesus do. I am now seeking the *true* treasure of the kingdom—peace. Peace beats recognition any day. "The Lord gives strength to his people; the Lord blesses his people with peace" (Ps. 29:11).

I am finding my peace, my satisfaction in him. Hope Chapel Red Lodge exists because I stopped waiting to be told what to do by men and followed my Lord. I abide by the bylaws of the denomination I chose to affiliate myself with and seek godly counsel when making big decisions, but ultimately, where and when I serve my Lord, and when I am served (spiritually fed) is up to me. And in the end, I alone will be accountable as to how I followed my Savior and fulfilled the plan he had for me. That choice to be the barbarian and conquer that which was set before me by my Lord—no more and no less—has indeed brought a deep-down satisfaction that can never be replicated by anything man would concoct, and it is my passion to equip and set others free to do the same—hence this writing.

Peace

We must find our strength in him and remain firmly in the kingdom where his will is done. The barbarian outside of the kingdom, or outside of the will of God, lacks peace. Without the peace of the Lord, the "peace of God, which surpasses all understanding" (Phil. 4:7 NKJV)—inner peace of the soul—we lose sight of our Lord and our place in the kingdom. When we lose sight of the Lord that peace can slip, and so will we. The appetites of the flesh take us over and we turn once again to the things which can bring us a temporary fix, a distraction at best, but never a peace.

The peace found in the strength of the Lord allows us to find a true and fulfilling satisfaction, a pure joy in the simple things in life: family, the love of a spouse, the laughter of children, a warm home, a full belly, a good cup of coffee . . . We too often think we need so much to be satisfied. The barbarians lived a pretty simple life but often their appetites for more drove them to the pillage, rape, and plunder thing. The appetite of the untamed heart can be a ravenous and terrible thing.

You know what ended the reign of terror for the Vikings, those infamous barbarians from the North? Christianity in large part. It's a long and complicated story and a lot if it is lost in obscurity, but when the gospel message of Jesus Christ reached into the hearts of the Norsemen, they found the fulfillment and peace they had been seeking and striving for since their ancestors first wandered away from the true God.

The churches, which first drew them to distant shores with their hoards of gold and silver, would later reveal a richer treasure as those within the church who had a heart for Jesus began to break through the hardened hearts of the raiders. What shields and swords could not accomplish, the sword of the Spirit, the gospel of peace, did. When the message of redemption began to take hold in the hearts of the Scandinavians, it took hold in a big way. It didn't happen overnight, but eventually the barbarians of the north shunned their war gods Odin, Loki, Thor or Woden, and Freyja—and a whole host of others—gods we still memorialize in the names of our days Wednesday, Thursday, and Friday on our western pagan barbarian- influenced calendar.

The cultures that spawned the Vikings turned away from the gods of war who demanded blood and doled out only strife—gods who rewarded bravery in battle with an eternity in the feasting hall of Valhalla, drinking by night and fighting by day in a never-ending cycle of debauchery and bloodshed—and turned to a God who is love. A God who promises peace, a peace found in the strength offered by a Savior who was brave and strong enough to conquer death itself. This peace that could satisfy even the most ravenous appetite, kind of put a whole different perspective on life—a God who would suffer for me, as opposed to one who demands that I suffer at his pleasure, might be worth listening to.

They started living in peace with their neighbors and became traders and tradesmen, shepherds and farmers, working hard and raising strong families. Think about that for a minute. Jesus satisfied the ravenous insatiable appetite of a people who would embrace a mythology that taught that the reward for dying in battle—literally dying with a sword in your hand—was that you would be allowed to cross over a bridge made of swords to a place where you would hack one another to pieces all day long, then spend the night drinking and feasting with those you had fought and killed, or maybe been killed by, as they would come back to life just to do it all over again the next day—this was Viking heaven!

The mindset that "never-ending battle and drunken feasting" was a reward to strive for speaks to the hunger in the barbarian soul for a satisfaction that can never be found in this life outside of the kingdom of God. The hunger that drives one to believe that "If I can only fight and show my bravery in battle, eat and drink to my heart's content forever, then maybe, just maybe, I will be satisfied, I will have peace"—is a hunger indeed. It is a passion that must be and should be *harnessed* for the kingdom of God; otherwise it will only destroy us.

I can relate to this. Back when I was living to party, I had this fantasy of just going on a running drunk, taking a week or two and just hitting the road, drinking and smoking all day and night, a non-stop party. Then maybe it would *finally* be enough, maybe I could reach that place of satisfaction I craved. There are people who have done that (gone on extended benders) and are still on them. I ministered to many of them in Billings. We have given them the politically correct title of *vagrants*, but many are indeed lost souls who have lost or given up everything in pursuit of the next high, answering to no one and being responsible to no one. Yet they are never satisfied; it is still never enough—and it will always become too much. An addict never gets enough of their drug of choice, even up to the point where it destroys them.

Many of us are still living in the dark ages and living for the mead hall experience, whether you're addicted to meds prescribed by your expensive doctor or holding a cardboard sign till you get enough money to buy a bottle, that desire to finally find peace is never ending and unquenchable in anything but our Lord, the true God who still holds his hand out offering strength to any who would look up and receive it. He is the living water and all who drink will never thirst again. Everything else is a lie and a false god, always teasing and enticing but never satisfying.

The pagan gods toyed with men, used them and abused them for their own amusement, rewarding them if they groveled and tolerated enough misery to impress them. Our God—the God of Abraham, Isaac, and Jacob, the God who came to this earth as a man through Jesus, born of a virgin in a sheep shelter and raised by a poor carpenter—is the Creator of the universe, the Creator of this earth, a place he created as a home for us, not so that we could give him amusement and stroke his ego, but so that we could be loved and blessed by him.

Why would we not find fulfillment in the heart of a God who created us to be one with him? Why would he go through all the trouble to create this world for us, to create us, to put up with us in our rebellion and foolishness, to come to this earth and die for us, just to leave us twisting in the wind, frustrated and hungry? He wouldn't, and he didn't. "Peace I leave with you; my peace I give you. I do not give to you as the world gives. Do not let your hearts be troubled and do not be afraid" (John 14:27).

A blessed man

Years ago, I heard from someone who was in a position of authority over me and under whom I had served for many years, these words: "If you leave this way I cannot bless you." This was in response to my announcement that I was pursuing my call to plant a new church.

There is a much larger context and longer story here obviously, but the point is, this really disturbed me. I had to decide: Am I going to do what I had always done—submit, work my tail off at someone else's direction and for their approval, or am I going to listen to and trust my Lord that no matter how difficult the road ahead, or who may be trying to call me off my God-given mission of conquest? Am I going to unchain myself from the oar I had been pulling on for so long in the bowels of the big stable Trireme? (The triple-decked, slave- driven ships the Greeks used.) Or am I going to stand in the helm of the sleek wind-driven longship and head to uncharted waters with the Lord plotting my course? I listened to my Lord and left without the blessing. But I found that the spray in my face, the wind at my back, and a boat full of fellow warriors who were just waiting for the freedom to be adventurers is a blessing that no man can impart—*it must be claimed.*

Yes, I am indeed a blessed man, blessed of God. I have joked several times over the last few years, "Who knew you had to plant a church to be rid of stress, to find peace?" Now, I wouldn't recommend church planting as therapy for a troubled heart, it just worked for me because I was doing exactly what my Lord had asked me to do, what he had purposed and prepared me to do, and I was being empowered and blessed by him in return. I was fulfilling his plan for my life—no more, no less—and I have found a strength and a peace in that. In that simple act of obedience to his voice, he set me on a journey that is fulfilling beyond words.

I came to Red Lodge with the barbarian determination of spirit, a singularity of mission, and a simplicity of purpose and planted a church for Jesus; *Hope Chapel.* We didn't, and we don't, play games or pretend that we are anybody we are not and we just love people. We love people for who they are just as Jesus does and give them the freedom to grow in him even if that growth takes them elsewhere. If it does, we send them out with a blessing—*no one* leaves Hope Chapel to serve or follow the Lord without a blessing.

I genuinely love the people who call Hope Chapel Red Lodge their family and I am indeed blessed to be their *barbarian* pastor.

Be the barbarian, listen to God, and conquer—no, be more than the conqueror . . .

"No, in all these things we are more than conquerors through him who loved us. For I am convinced that neither death nor life, neither angels nor demons, neither the present nor the future, nor any powers, neither height nor depth, nor anything else in all creation, will be able to separate us from the love of God that is in Christ Jesus our Lord" (Rom. 8:37–39).

My family and I have come ashore, conquered, and settled in a good land where we have been blessed with health, fruitfulness, and adventure—all a barbarian family really needs.

the BARBARIAN council

We should not make it difficult for the Gentiles who are turning to God. (Acts 15:19)

BY NOW I hope you have come to have a new understanding of, and even embraced the title *Barbarians in the Kingdom*, because that would be us. In fact, that would be just about everyone who is not a descendant of Abraham, and who has put their faith in Jesus. To the Romans, the barbarians were those living beyond the frontiers of the empire; to the Israelite, everyone else was a barbarian, or in their vernacular, a *Gentile*. Ironically, to the Jew, even those with whom the word originated—*(barbarus)* the Romans—were considered barbarians. And not without cause, for all their technological advances and sophistication, the Romans were heavy-handed pagan tyrants who had invaded their land and ruled by the edge of the sword.

With two millennia separating us from the birth of the church at Pentecost, we, the Gentile barbarians, take it for granted that we are welcome into the kingdom with little thought or regard as to how we got there and what a stir this caused both in the heavens and amongst

God's chosen people—the Israelites. Prior to the death and resurrection of our Lord and the subsequent outpouring of the Holy Spirit, the *elect* were a pretty small and elite group. In fact, it was those people to whom, and through whom, the Messiah came. "You know the message God sent to the people of Israel, announcing the good news of peace through Jesus Christ, who is Lord of all" (Acts 10:36).

It wasn't that God didn't want all people to know him. Primarily, it was the case that nearly all of mankind—person after person, clan after clan, tribe after tribe, all the way back to the great flood—had wandered away from the true God, save for one notable exception, Abraham. Abraham (or Abram) held on to the knowledge of the truth that somehow had been handed down to him and he continued to worship the Creator of the heavens and the earth. So God chose him to be the keeper of a covenant. Abraham and his descendants, who would become the nation of Israel, would be entrusted with the stories, the Law, and the covenant promises of redemption and renewal that would ultimately lead to the coming of the Messiah, who would be the new Adam by whom all people would be saved as they inherited his righteousness. Just as in the first Adam all people were lost as they inherited his sinfulness.

With the coming of the Messiah, the Israelites were now entrusted as the keepers of a *new* covenant, a fulfillment really of the old covenant that started with Abraham, found its fullness through Moses with the written law, and now finds its fulfillment in Jesus of Nazareth, the Son of God and Man. But there was a problem: The Israelites to whom Jesus had come and made the purveyors of the new covenant were not too keen on sharing it with the Gentiles. This was *their* God, this was *their* Messiah; after all, hadn't God commanded them to separate themselves from all those barbarians? "You are well aware that it is against our law for a Jew to associate with or visit a Gentile. But God has shown me that I should not call anyone impure or unclean" (Acts 10:28).

God wanted to segregate Israel, not because he didn't want them to be a light and a witness of him to the world, but because the opposite always seemed to happen. Israel had a long history of getting themselves into big trouble whenever they found themselves mingling with the nations around them. So the Jewish followers of Jesus were not too sure what to do with this new command from their Lord to make disciples of all nations. ("Therefore go and make disciples of all nations" Matt. 28:19). This was a huge paradigm shift and they still weren't sure how all this grace business related to the law they had lived by for so long. This was a quandary; there was no way they could get all these pagan idol worshippers to even began to understand the law of God, let alone live by it. But God had another plan, and he was about to rock the boat—big time.

The vision

One day while praying, Peter, the fisherman turned apostle, had a vision of a huge sheet being let down from heaven, containing animals of all sorts. Notably to Peter, these were all the animals the Israelites had been commanded they must never eat: pigs, reptiles, birds . . . Peter, suddenly very hungry, was told to get up, "kill and eat," but he refused. This happened three times until the Spirit said to him: "Do not call anything impure that God has made clean" (Acts 10:15). Then the vision ended, leaving Peter perplexed—and still hungry.

But Peter was about to find out what this meant; he was headed to a barbarian smorgasbord for lunch.

Enter Cornelius

While Peter was still thinking about the vision, the Spirit said to him, "Simon, three men are looking for you. So get up and go downstairs. Do not hesitate to go with them, for I have sent them."

Peter went down and said to the men, "I'm the one you're looking for. Why have you come?"

The men replied, "We have come from Cornelius the centurion. He is a righteous and God-fearing man, who is respected by all the Jewish people. A holy angel told him to ask you to come to his house so that he could hear what you have to say." (Acts 10:19–22)

Peter, an Israelite by birth and an apostle to the Jewish Messiah—*Son of David* and *Son of God*—was being asked to go, not just to a Gentile's house, but to a Roman's house. God is about to blow down the gates to the kingdom and Peter doesn't know it yet, but he does indeed have the key to that kingdom gate just as Jesus said he would.

This is not easy for Peter—for any Jew. The Romans are not just their enemy, they are vicious coldblooded invaders who kill anyone who gets in their way. Peter had just watched them crucify his Lord a few short weeks earlier. They desecrate everything holy to the Jews. Just a few years ago, they had hung a Roman standard above the walls of the temple, huge banners bearing the image of a Caesar who had proclaimed himself a god. Pilate, the new Roman governor come to ensure Jewish subjugation to Rome, had hung these in the night and this blasphemy greeted the worshippers in the temple courtyard at sunrise—a graven image breaking the very first of the Ten Commandments.

When the people complained, Pilate made a pretense of wanting to hear them out and set a meeting. But when the crowd had gathered in the courtyard of his villa, he turned his centurions and their soldiers loose on the unarmed and defenseless crowd, surrounding them and threatening to slaughter them. It was a threat not to be taken lightly as many massacres of innocents had already been suffered by the Jews at the hands of these Roman storm troopers.

More often than not, the traveler to Jerusalem was greeted by the gruesome sight of the tortured dead and dying hanging along the roadside on the wooden crosses the Romans were so fond of using. They were a horror and a warning to all of what happens if you dare question or cross the ultimate authority of Rome. Imagine if we had lost world War II and our streets were now patrolled by the dreaded SS and we were forced to have a swastika hanging in our churches—that's what the centurion and his legions were to the Jew, enforcers of blasphemy. Now Peter is being asked to go to the home of one of these barbarians, a Roman centurion, to tell them about Jesus—the man they had crucified as though it was just another day at work.

For thousands of years the Israelites had been abused, enslaved, attacked, and harassed by the nations all around them, as they still are today. To the Jew they are all barbarians. "Surely, Lord, you can't be serious. You want me to talk to—*the Romans?*" To go into their house, eat their profane food, drink their wine, and give them the treasures of heaven in return?" Little did Peter, or any of them, know that this was just the beginning. Jesus had, after all, said: "Therefore go and make disciples of *all* nations" (Matt. 28:19). But the *Romans?* "Lord, can't I just head north and find some Germanic tree worshippers to preach to? At least those barbarians have kept to themselves in their wilderness villages."

But Peter, to his credit, obeys the Holy Spirit and goes to the Roman's house. After hearing, from Cornelius, the story about how God had spoken to him at the very same time Peter was having his own vision of the "meat lovers non-kosher banquet," he shares the gospel with Cornelius and his family.

Preaching to the Gentiles

> Then Peter opened his mouth and said: "In truth I perceive that God shows no partiality. But in every nation whoever fears Him and works righteousness is accepted by Him. . . . The word which God sent to the children of Israel, preaching peace through Jesus Christ—He is Lord of all— . . .

To Him all the prophets witness that, through His name, whoever believes in Him will receive remission of sins."

While Peter was still speaking these words, the Holy Spirit fell upon all those who heard the word. And those of the circumcision who believed were astonished, as many as came with Peter, because the gift of the Holy Spirit had been poured out on the Gentiles also. For they heard them speak with tongues and magnify God.

Then Peter answered, "Can anyone forbid water, that these should not be baptized who have received the Holy Spirit just as we have?" And he commanded them to be baptized in the name of the Lord. Then they asked him to stay a few days. (Acts 10:34–36, 43–48 NKJV)

Thus the gates of the kingdom are thrown wide open—let the pillaging begin.

This scene would be repeated time and again from Africa to Asia, the Mediterranean to the British Isles and India, as the apostles and early disciples, the Jewish followers of Christ, were scattered and sent to all the corners of the world with the message of Jesus Christ.

"The Holy Spirit fell upon all those who heard the word" (Acts 10:44 NKJV). No hocus pocus, emotionally charged, anointing oil slathered carnival, no tarrying and fasting, no classes and studies—they heard the Word, they believed, and they received. That's why I have often prayed for people in my church to receive the baptism of the Spirit even from the pulpit to where they sit *en masse*. If they are willing to receive, they will. I do prefer the one on one laying on of hands, but ultimately I try to follow the Spirit's lead.

"The Holy Spirit fell" on them when they heard the Word; Jesus Christ is the same yesterday, today and forever—Jesus didn't change his mind and retract the Holy Spirit or make him harder to receive. He gives the Spirit to all who ask. If a son asks his father for a fish, will he instead give him a serpent (see Luke 11:11).

Not our show

By pouring out his Spirit on the centurion and his family, Jesus was showing his disciples that *all* are now welcome. This was God's show, this was *his* church and he was building it the way it was supposed to be built—by getting his people out there to share the good news and leaving the rest up to him. "Get out of my way and watch me work!" No religion, no rituals, just come and receive—be freed. People don't radically change because they hear a new set of rules they like. They change because something happens inside, because the Holy Spirit is poured out. I know because it happened to me. Jesus died so we could receive his life-changing, life-giving Spirit. That's why I am a *barbarian with a Bible,* instead of just a barbarian with an insatiable appetite, or just another plastic Christian.

The Father was calling his children—all his children—home. Because of this, the peoples who had for so long rejected and had so long ago abandoned faith in the one true God were now being reconciled in droves. All of them with no knowledge whatsoever of the Law or the prophets. They had no Bible—the New Testament was still hundreds of years from being canonized. If they were lucky, they had a copy of a letter from one of the apostles or a written account of the life and teachings of Jesus that would become one of the Gospels—but the one thing they all had was the power, the life-giving, life-changing power of the Holy Spirit poured out on them when they believed. At which point the law became "written on their hearts."

The very thing the law was intended to accomplish when it was handed down to the Israelites at Mt. Sinai so long ago was happening: People were treating one another with love and respect. They were forsaking selfishness in exchange for selflessness, despair for hope, fear for courage, weakness for strength. They shunned all other gods and worshipped the Creator, who was now living in their hearts and calling them children. "In the last days, God says, I will pour out my Spirit on all people. Your sons and daughters will prophesy, your young men will see visions, your old men will dream dreams" (Acts 2:17).

God was speaking, and the barbarian was listening.

The barbarian council

But not everyone was happy with this situation. The kingdom of God was being overrun by the uncivilized and unwashed masses who had no clue what it meant to live a holy life, who didn't have the proper respect for the traditions or knowledge of the requirements of the law. At least this was what a good many of the Jewish followers of Jesus thought.

You can't really blame them, this was a huge change and a big challenge. Those who had tied up their entire identity for eons as a people who adhered to a very specific and strict code of religion and ritual, were now being asked to embrace the heathen. The barbarian was waltzing out of the woods all bright-eyed and bushytailed right into the kingdom like they had never committed a sin in their short miserable lives. And now they just expected to be partakers of the riches of heaven like those who had earned it? *I don't think so!*

Again, God had another plan. It was time for the Barbarian Council.

Bible scholars like to refer to this meeting as the *Jerusalem Council,* but the express purpose of this council of church elders meeting in Jerusalem was to determine what to do with the barbarian hordes that were now storming into the kingdom.

> Certain people came down from Judea to Antioch and were teaching the believers: "Unless you are circumcised, according to the custom taught by Moses, you cannot be saved." This brought Paul and Barnabas into sharp dispute and debate with them. So Paul and Barnabas were appointed, along with some other believers, to go up to Jerusalem to see the apostles and elders about this question. (Acts 15:1–2)

The barbarian and Greek influx into the kingdom forced the Jewish leaders of the church to look at the relationship between the Law and the believer, to make the distinction once and for all between the old and new covenants. And God chose a very unlikely person to represent the Gentiles and their disputed position in the kingdom: Paul, a Pharisee turned apostle. The same man who would later write of the kingdom: "Here there is no Gentile or Jew, circumcised or uncircumcised, barbarian, Scythian, slave or free, but Christ is all, and is in all. Therefore, as God's chosen people, holy and dearly loved, clothe yourselves with compassion, kindness, humility, gentleness and patience" (Col. 3:11–12).

This was no small thing for a Jew and former Pharisee to write. Israel was *the chosen people*, the children of Abraham to whom belong the riches of the kingdom. The Israelites must have thought, "We are the ones who have suffered, worked, and patiently waited." But God had taken Paul, a Jew of Jews and a Pharisee of Pharisees, poured out his Spirit on him, and opened his eyes to the truth of *all* the Scriptures, the laws and the prophecies that he had so diligently studied and memorized, and showed him that it had all been pointing to, and leading up to, this day. It all pointed to this day when all would be welcome into the kingdom by virtue of the sacrifice of God's Son. By grace we would be saved through faith, not by works, lest any man should boast!

Paul now finds himself as God's chosen man to press the apostles—as the authoritative representatives of Jesus Christ—to make an edict once and for all as to what exactly is required of the Gentile believers, of *all* believers—Jewish, Greek, Roman, Scythian, barbarian, as regards the law of Moses. So the apostle Paul comes to Jerusalem to appeal to the leaders of the church there, most notably James the brother of Jesus, along with John, and Peter, because the new Gentile believers in Antioch were being told they must receive circumcision in order to be accepted by God. In other words, to make themselves subject to the old covenant with all its laws and requirements.

A council is convened, and the matter is debated. Simon Peter—the man who first witnessed the Holy Spirit being poured out on the heathen Romans but more recently had been wavering on the grace versus the law issue—suddenly finds his voice once again after hearing a group of Messianic Pharisees argue for forcing the law onto the barbarians. Perhaps hearing their arguments stirred in his heart memories of his Jesus castigating the Pharisees time and again for piling burdens on people that no one could ever bear. Peter's argument is worth reading in its entirety:

> After much discussion, Peter got up and addressed them: "Brothers, you know that some time ago God made a choice among you that the Gentiles might hear from my lips the message of the gospel and believe. God, who knows the heart, showed that he accepted them by giving the Holy Spirit to them, just as he did to us. He did not discriminate between us and them, for he purified their hearts by faith. Now then, why do you try to test God by putting on the necks of Gentiles a yoke that neither we nor our ancestors have been able to bear? No! We believe it is through the grace of our Lord Jesus that we are saved, just as they are."
>
> The whole assembly became silent as they listened to Barnabas and Paul telling about the signs and wonders God had done among the Gentiles through them. When they finished, James spoke up. "Brothers," he said, "listen to me. Simon has described to us how God first intervened to choose a people for his name from the Gentiles. The words of the prophets are in agreement with this, as it is written:
>
> "'After this I will return and rebuild David's fallen tent. Its ruins I will rebuild, and I will restore it, that the rest of mankind may seek the Lord, even all the Gentiles who bear my name, says the Lord, who does these things—things known from long ago.'
>
> "It is my judgment, therefore, that we should not make it difficult for the Gentiles who are turning to God." (Acts 15:7–19)

Peter's impassioned and Spirit-inspired argument prevails, and in the end a letter is composed to settle the matter once and for all. It is sealed and given to Paul and Barnabas to take back to Antioch where it is read to the barbarian church. In the verses to follow, we find the text of that letter containing a list of *all the laws* they were obliged to follow in order to live holy lives; an exhaustive and comprehensive rundown of what is required to be upstanding citizens of the kingdom of their God. Here is that list:

> The apostles and elders, your brothers,
> To the Gentile believers in Antioch, Syria and Cilicia:
> Greetings.
> It seemed good to the Holy Spirit and to us not to burden you with anything beyond the following requirements: You are to abstain from food sacrificed to idols, from blood, from the meat of strangled animals and from sexual immorality. You will do well to avoid these things. Farewell (Acts 15:23, 28–29)

That's it, all that the law required from the new believers summed up in one sentence, in essence—be careful what you eat, and keep your pants on. Seems like a strange requirement but these things all had to do with worshipping pagan gods. So basically, they were being told: "Worship the one true God and him alone."

This decision by the apostles and elders as to what was required of the barbarians entering the kingdom would become the impetus and focus of Paul's writings, the letters he wrote to the churches explaining how the Gentiles are now to live in their newly discovered grace. These letters were of course to become our Scriptures as they form much of the New Testament, which is why Paul would later write: "I am a debtor both to Greeks and to barbarians, both to wise and to unwise. So, as much as is in me, I am ready to preach the gospel to you who are in Rome also" (Rom. 1:14–15 NKJV).

The "holier than thou" opposition of the religious and the civilized to the Spirit-filled barbarians forced the issue with the church leaders. Paul had to take up where Peter had left off and basically saved the church from being sucked right back into the religious—the ritual and rule-based—system that Jesus had so adamantly taught against and died to free us from. If not for the barbarians pressing at the gates of the kingdom, eager to take part in the riches of God's goodness and power, the followers of Jesus might just have become a fringe sect of Judaism, bereft of all power, having the truth once again shrouded in an impenetrable cloak of largely manmade ritual, liturgy, and sacraments—as it has in some quarters of the Christian church anyway.

But *simplicity of purpose* prevailed and freedom was thus ordained.

Freedom

The barbarian way of life, the driving force, the reason they fought and resisted the Roman onslaught and the Greek invasion before that, the reason they lived in the north where the civilized were afraid or ill-prepared and unwilling to survive, was because they cherished above most all other virtues—freedom. Freedom to live, love, and laugh; freedom to be who they were; freedom to work, sweat, and bleed to better their lot for themselves and their families. Even the freedom to fail and to die in the trying was better than slavery in the wealthiest house.

Theirs was a love of the creation that both challenged and rewarded them when they met that challenge. And now they were being offered another level of freedom by the very God who created it all, and them—Jesus. Jesus the Jewish Messiah, a man who was crucified by the civilized purveyors of a religion that seemingly offered *anything but* freedom, was now offering freedom. Freedom from the one thing they still feared and could not overcome by the sword—death. Always, death came for all of them no matter how bravely they fought and lived. Their legends of what lay beyond was a mystery shrouded in an enigma, and their superstitions of gods and powers beyond their comprehension and control were a constant threat that weighed heavily on the barbarian heart.

Then along comes these Hebrew vagrants, exiles from their own land and people telling them of a man who claimed to be a *Son of God*, who overcame death and proved it by walking out of the tomb, three days dead and cold, now alive and well. A God become a man, who offered not a meager hope of just another day to toil and strive hoping to find favor in the sight of another petty and spiteful god, but eternal life, a chance to be forgiven for everything they have ever done that their hearts and better instincts had told them was wrong. Here was a God offering peace and reconciliation with the Creator of the heavens and the earth. And to prove it, his Spirit was being poured out on them in tangible ways that they could see, hear, and feel, simply for the asking, giving them a hope not just for the next life, but for this one as well. Here indeed was true freedom.

The barbarian heart thrives in the freedom of our Lord and in the power of his Holy Spirit. The very kingdom of God thrives in the heart of the barbarian, the *Barbarian with a Bible*. That Bible being made up of the letters that the apostles who took part in that first *barbarian council* wrote to the churches that were springing up far and wide amongst the Gentile barbarians, ensuring that the message of freedom that brings peace and hope, strength, courage, and freedom to all people would not be forgotten, lost, or perverted.

> "So those who rely on faith are blessed along with Abraham, the man of faith. For all who rely on the works of the law are under a curse, as it is written: 'Cursed is everyone who does not continue to do everything written in the Book of the Law.' Clearly no one who relies on the law is justified before God, because 'the righteous will live by faith'" (Gal. 3:9–11).

The New Testament, the words written to confirm and verify that the freedom of the new law—the law of love, joy, peace, patience, goodness, kindness, gentleness, faithfulness, and self-control—would not be lost or swallowed up ever again by religious demands and burdens that we, the mighty uncivilized, fearsome and untamed barbarian, could not carry or tolerate. The barbarian heart cannot thrive for long in the shackles of religion. God knows this, the apostles knew this, and if you are honest with yourself—you know this. As we allow ourselves to get civilized and sophisticated, we lose sight of this. That is why the church is slowly but surely fading away, and that is why we need barbarians to stand up and say: "*Enough!* I am who I am; I am a child of God and I am free! I have the Word of God written on my heart and on my mind. I have the Spirit of the living God empowering my soul to overcome my flesh and the enemy, and I have a Bible, the sword of the Spirit, and I'm not afraid to use it!"

We need to tell that religious spirit that threatens to destroy us, "Take your rules and condemnations, your demands and your never-ending circular and meaningless theologies, your 'my way is right and your way is wrong' methodologies, and take a long walk off a short pier because my ship is no longer tied to your pier. My ship is following the *King of Kings* and the *Lord of Lords* to the Promised Land, but first we are going to stop at the gates of hell where we are going to kick butt and set the captives free!"

Maybe we need another Barbarian Council; I think the Holy Spirit is already there and the invitations have been sent—"Come to me, all you who are weary and burdened and I will give you rest" (Matt. 11:28 NKJV). Bottom line is, God is extending his hand to all peoples, "*Come home, my children, barbarians and all.*"

CHAPTER 7

MY SOUL, MY SWORD, MY SERVICE TO MY KING

We must obey God rather than human beings! (Acts 5:29b)

THROUGHOUT THIS WRITING I have made several allusions to the effect that the reason I have come to be considered somewhat of a barbarian is because I have been very selective in whom I choose to listen to—whom I submit to—and bold in my dedication and desire to follow the Lord as best as I can down the path that he lays before me. The very notion I have laid out as the driving motivation behind the barbarian, that of "simplicity of purpose, singularity of mission, and determination of spirit," could give one the impression that the barbarian is wholly independent and self-determining in his pursuits.

Yes, it is important to not get sidetracked or outright derailed in our pursuits, but that is predicated on the premise that our pursuits are guided by the Lord and are part of his plan for our lives. This plan can be revealed to us by his Holy Spirit and by his Word. But the Lord often uses others to speak into our lives as well: prophets, teachers, pastors, loved ones, and brothers and sisters in the Lord. We are part of a family and must function as a family.

The barbarians of old were fiercely independent and cherished freedom, but they also had a strong sense of honor and that honor was nowhere more important than in keeping the oaths they made. Those oaths were the glue that held their communities and their war-bands together as they gave their allegiance and their swords over to a person, e.g., a king, a jarl, or a lord, who had earned their trust and respect. By submitting to the authority of another, they could work together, and in unison, toward a single goal, whether it be keeping a community safe from enemies or conquering new lands and waters. To keep a village, a longship, or a kingdom solvent and prospering, someone had to be in command and have the final say.

When the barbarians turned to the living God and gave their oaths to Jesus Christ as the final say in their lives, they did so wholeheartedly, knowing their honor was still at stake and when they made that commitment there would be no turning back and no being dissuaded by any other voices. Yes, there would still need to be more earthly authorities in their lives to maintain order and cohesion, but those voices would always be secondary to that of the true King. That, I believe, is where we in the *civilized* church of today have gotten a bit off track. We have given authorities in the church—spiritual leaders—the authority over us that only God should have. We have given our oaths too hastily and severely limited ourselves, and God, in the process.

And church leaders have been all too eager to solicit, and accept, those oaths. So if you will indulge me for a bit, I will attempt in the final pages here at the end of our barbarian adventure to bring some light and balance to a very big topic—*submission*. Scripture does have a lot to say about this indeed. Let's start with the one many of you may have been screaming at me in your heads (or maybe out loud) throughout your reading of this book.

To the elders among you, I appeal as a fellow elder and a witness of Christ's sufferings who also will share in the glory to be revealed: Be shepherds of God's flock that is under your care, watching over them—not because you must, but because you are willing, as God wants you to be; not pursuing dishonest gain, but eager to serve; not lording it over those entrusted to you, but being examples to the flock. And when the Chief Shepherd appears, you will receive the crown of glory that will never fade away. In the same way, you who are younger, submit yourselves to your elders. All of you, clothe yourselves with humility toward one another, because: "God opposes the proud but shows favor to the humble." (1 Peter 5:1–5)

" . . . you who are younger, *submit*. . . ." There's that word, big and bold. Church is really about the only place you hear this word anymore because it's not a word that people want to hear. There's a little thing called pride that gets in the way. "You can't tell me what to do, you're not the boss of me!" To insist on someone submitting to us is to invite rebellion and animosity—especially if we use that word. It's not in our nature to want to submit and it seems like such a harsh word unless we understand that submitting is really nothing more than respecting authority.

Submitting to someone requires a level of trust and humility. It's a big thing to give another person the right to give us direction or to accept their rebuke. This happens in the workplace all the time, it has to or nothing would get done. If everyone did whatever they felt like whenever they wanted with no one held responsible for anything, the company would soon go out of business, unless of course you work for the federal government—but they get to print their own money and make up their own rules. For the rest of us, this just doesn't work.

We're gonna die!
Certainly, in the world of construction where I work there must always be someone in charge, not just to get things done but to keep everyone safe. I learned this early on in my illustrious construction

career. One day in my eighteenth summer, I found myself in the Job Corps heavy equipment training program running a D-8 Cat (a really big bulldozer) on a mountainside outside of Butte, Montana. We were cutting in a road for the forest service. The instructors were old union hands from the rough and tumble town of Butte, and they could cuss you out in more ways than you ever dreamed possible and tell you stories from their SEABEE days in WWII and Korea that made you glad to just be pushing dirt in Montana even if you *were* hanging off the side of a mountain.

Anyway, speaking of hanging off a mountain, on this day that's what I was doing, making the first cut on a very steep hillside that would become a road. So here I am, pushing rocks, trees and dirt; leaning sideways in the seat while keeping close track of two things: the instructor on the ground, Clint, who was guiding my every move and . . . I was paying close attention to the bubble in my rear end. Our instructors had another name for the location of this bubble but I can't use it in polite company although you will find the term in the King James Bible, in reference to a donkey.

They said all good operators had to have this bubble in their . . . burro. Basically it's like the bubble in a level that tells you how far you need to adjust something to get to level. A good operator has to know just by feel when he is level or when he is getting too close to tipping over. My bubble was serving me well that day and I was comfortable with what we were doing, and I trusted the instructor who was watching and guiding me—I was submitted.

Actually, the main reason I remember this day so well is because of the sheer panic of the guy riding with me in the "buddy seat," Frank, a farm kid from North Dakota. The cat had a seat bolted to the top of the fuel tank next to the operator's seat, putting it a couple of feet higher than the operator. All the equipment had buddy seats so that the newer guys could ride along with the more experienced hands and watch how they did things.

From his perch there on the downhill side of our side-hilling adventure, his bubble was telling him we were going to die and he made no bones about letting me know. While I was concentrating on the instructor's signals, he was literally beating on my shoulder and screaming, "We're gonna die, we're gonna die!" Well, neither one of us died that day and Frank, who no longer cared much to ride with me, eventually made it back home safe and sound to the great plains of North Dakota where things are nice and level.

On this day, I was glad I listened to the instructor; I learned a lot about what both I and this big cat could do and I was also learning to trust my bubble, even getting it fine-tuned—calibrated. If I had listened to the guy screaming in my ear, I would have missed all that. I would not have learned to trust the instructor, the *elder*, and likewise, the instructor would not have come to trust me. This two-way trust was very important in my becoming an operator as I wouldn't always have someone watching and guiding my every move.

If I had listened to the wrong voice, like say, the guy beating on my arm and screaming in terror—or let him distract me, I might have even gotten us both hurt, or worse. None of the equipment we ran back then in the seventies had cabs or roll bars (protective cages around the operator). Our lives and limbs were protected by the bubble, our instincts, and our willingness to learn from and submit to our instructors.

Life doesn't have roll bars either

It's important that we learn to submit, that we know whom to trust and whom to listen to. But it's not always all that easy, it's not always black and white. We need to be always also paying attention to that inner bubble, our own instincts, and—in the case of the barbarian in the kingdom—the inner voice of the Holy Spirit. This is a real challenge and one that never goes away. It is in fact my refusing to blithely submit to an "elder" or two that got me branded with the barbarian moniker in the first place, landed me squarely in the middle of God's plan for me, and gave birth to my current teaching and writing ministry.

Before we proceed further I want to throw this out there for you to keep in mind as we explore this notion of submission, and I believe this insight comes straight from the Holy Spirit: We should respect authority in our lives and obey the Spirit of God, but do not confuse the two. You can be respectful to authority without offering blind and unquestioned obedience. As I have said before, we are disciples of Jesus Christ, not a pastor.

Submit!

Throughout life, from home, to school, to the workplace, I have had to learn to respect authority and have been told more than once, in all those places, that I must "listen" better. I'm somewhat ADD, not to mention stubborn (if you are wasting my time I have better places to go, even if it's only in my own mind). In the church, these admonitions are put in a different way, and more than once I was told, "You need to learn to submit."

For the most part I got pretty good at submitting, even to the point where I found myself doing things I didn't believe I was supposed to be doing, long after I thought I was supposed to be done doing them. But I was a good little servant, which is really not my nature, but I submitted to church leaders because I believed we had a biblical mandate to do so and because I wanted to learn how to *be* one. Just like I submitted to my Job Corps instructors because I wanted to become an operator like they were, and because they had earned my trust and respect long before that little mountainside adventure on the big cat—though I must admit I was rather enjoying scaring the pants off poor Frank.

I even got to the place where I was submissive to the point of spiritual co-dependency within the church, always seeking the approval and guidance of others. Ironic when I was still bucking authority most other places—perhaps *questioning* authority is a better description. I think it's important to ask the right questions and to know how to think for yourself, and in my construction career it has put me in a position of being a project superintendent for the company I work for. Then one day it hit me that I needed to take that initiative in the church as well. All of us at some point need to put on our big boy pants, be the barbarian, and just do what we know we are supposed to do, what we know deep in our gut is right. At some point that bubble in the rear end is as calibrated as it's going to be and we need to pay attention to it and make the proper adjustments.

Which brings me to our next submission verse: "So Christ himself gave the apostles, the prophets, the evangelists, the pastors and teachers, to equip his people for works of service, so that the body of Christ may be built up until we all reach unity in the faith and in the knowledge of the Son of God and become mature, attaining to the whole measure of the fullness of Christ" (Eph. 4:11–13).

This, like the exhortation from Peter that addressed the "younger," would seem to put a bit of a limit—a frame of reference—to the level of our submitting. We have the apostles, the prophets, the evangelists, pastors, and teachers to guide us, give us direction, equip us *until* (a very small but very significant qualifying word there), until we are mature in our unity in the faith and knowledge—until we are committed to attaining the fullness of Christ. In other words, (I believe) when we become true disciples of Christ.

When does this happen? Only you and the Lord can know that, and it will probably always be somewhat incremental, meaning most likely you will need to be doing both; always submitting, either directly to the Holy Spirit—the voice of the Holy Spirit in our own hearts—or sometimes through a person, a leader in the church whom God is using to shepherd us. And I don't have to tell you that if either of these voices run counter to the Scriptures you had better be double checking to see whose bubble is out of whack. The law may be written on our hearts but our hearts can be woefully deceitful, and so can the hearts of others. I don't believe the "fullness of Christ" we are to aspire to will come until we take the responsibility to discern and listen for the voice of the Spirit as our primary guide and pledge our obedience to him.

Ultimately, the choice of to whom and to what extent to give your oath is yours. And wisdom comes with maturity, but it does come. It must, because if we don't learn when, how, and to whom to submit, we can waste a lot of time—or worse, end up in a wreck.

Meanwhile back on the mountain

Back to my Job Corps days. A few weeks after that same project where I was cutting in a new road with that cat, I had another experience that ended a little differently.

This time I was running a big rubber-tired scraper at the other end of the road project. We were making a cut into a mountainside for the new road bed and hauling the dirt to a lower spot farther on, and again there was an instructor close by, Will. He was giving me signals as I came in for the cut. I dropped the *can* (the hopper that makes up the back half of the scraper) and just as the blade at the bottom of the can started to bite into the dirt like a giant carpenter's plane, the *push cat* (the bulldozer used to push the scraper as it gets bogged down while picking up its load of dirt) came in behind to push me as the can filled with dirt—a perfect maneuver by my good friend Ted, an Oglala Lakota Sioux from Porcupine Ridge, South Dakota. His bubble was working fine and he hit me at just the right speed just before I bogged down and lost momentum, and not so hard that I got whiplash.

I looked at Will and he was motioning me closer to the downhill edge, so I moved a little closer. He motioned me to go closer still, and I went a little closer still. Apparently it wasn't close enough and his signals were getting more pronounced, but I hesitated because my bubble was telling me that if I got any closer to the edge I was going over. Will was determined to override my bubble and I could see he was getting angry as he started motioning quite dramatically. I thought, "Fine, have it your way!" I went over where he wanted me and sure enough, I started going over—the right front wheel breaking through the fragile edge of the ledge we had been cutting.

Fortunately, all the times I had had it drilled into my head by the instructors that if you ever got in trouble on whatever you are running "drop the bucket or the blade as hard and as fast as you can" was now instinct and I did just that. I shoved that can control lever forward as hard as I could, lowering the can and causing the blade to bite deeply into the ground. About this time, Will started waving at Ted, who was still pushing me with the fill cat. Ted hadn't seen the front half of the articulated scraper going over because he was focused on the tail of that scraper (called the stinger) where his blade was doing its work. When he saw Will waving at him and pointing down—meaning "Drop your blade and stop!"— he thought Will was trying to get him to look down at his gauges, so in the meantime he just kept pushing me right over the edge.

But this actually worked in my favor. By the time he realized he needed to stop, the front half of the scraper—the part where I was sitting—was completely sideways, hanging off the mountainside, but the can was buried so deep that I wasn't going anywhere. I was firmly anchored.

Ted sat there on that old Euclid cat wide-eyed and scared for me. I unbuckled my seat belt, climbed up on the left tire, which was now way up in the air, and jumped to the soft ground. I waved at Ted to let him know I was okay and then I sauntered down the slope to Will and said, "Well, I got over. Looks like we might need to go get the D-8 Cat to pull us out."

Will, who wasn't shy about expressing his opinion, especially if he thought you messed up, just said, "Yeah, you're probably right." So none of us having a vehicle around and having both pieces of equipment in somewhat precarious positions, I walked a mile or two to the other end of the job to where the big cat was working.

There are times to submit, and there are times that, maybe, it's just not the best idea.

I'm pretty sure that little episode was one that was on the minds of these old union hands months later when they explained to me why I was declined for the International Union of Operating Engineers (IUOE) apprenticeship program offered to some Job Corps graduates. It was decided that "I was too aggressive to be an apprentice" and that "I should go out as a journeyman." I guess my inner barbarian was showing. I was surprised to hear this because I usually thought of myself as shy and submissive, so I took this as a huge compliment. It meant that I had proven my mettle, earned their trust and respect, and was ready to go to work doing what I loved. I got there by listening, submitting to those in authority over me, and listening to my own instincts—trusting the bubble in my rear. I had earned respect by giving it. I had learned to submit without being a doormat.

Respect

We don't always get respect from those who demand it of us, though, do we? That's especially troublesome in the church. I hear people in the church all the time say to me—actually, not so much anymore since I have started encouraging people in my church to be disciples of Jesus rather than disciples of pastors—but I used to hear a lot: "I'm learning to submit." This often troubled me because it too often sounds like the words of a *slave* who has no say and is allowed no opinion about what he or she is supposed to be doing—a doormat—and that's just not right.

But we can't ignore or discount the whole notion of submitting to spiritual leaders. Learning to submit is important and biblically you can't get away from the fact that we are *supposed* to.

Have confidence in your leaders and submit to their authority . . . (Heb. 13:17).

You know that the household of Stephanas were the first converts in Achaia, and they have devoted themselves to the service of the Lord's people. I urge you, brothers and sisters, to submit to such people . . . (1 Cor. 16:15–16).

So I guess the real question here is, to whom? To whom, in the family of God, are we supposed to submit, when, and for how long? A casual reading of the verses we just looked at would suggest that we do a lot of submitting to a lot of people and it becomes a blanket we throw over the entire leadership structure of the church that covers all situations and all aspects of our lives in Christ. I think this is a gross misunderstanding and it has crippled the average Christian and put undue pressure on the leadership.

A closer look at the context of these verses in the chapters they are in, and at the Scriptures as a whole, reveal that the submission of believers to those given authority is a very tricky, and actually quite limited, proposition. Ultimately, I think it comes down to this: Legitimate authority is God given and must be kept in balance by the Spirit of God. Any abuse or misuse will have to be answered for by both the one leading and the one who allowed himself, or herself, to be misled.

We all have the same Holy Spirit (our spiritual bubble to guide us) and access to the same Holy Scriptures. And no matter who we are asked to submit to, we all will have to answer to God, now, and in the end.

107

We must get past the tradition of blind submission and take an honest look at the heart of the scriptures concerning this issue. Submission is biblical so I am not here to tell you to rebel but we need to keep this concept in a healthy perspective.

If the verses we have looked at are being used to beat down and hamstring the people chosen and called by God, then they are being abused. Leaders who will not allow people to use the gifts the Spirit gave them to pursue the passions God has given them to make an impact on the kingdom of God, are doing the kingdom and its warriors a huge disservice. Every church leader has a responsibility to protect their ministry and prayerfully select that which will enhance it; but they do not have the right to hamper another from following the Lord *outside* of that area. That's not a submission issue; that's a control issue—that is overstepping the authority granted to them by God.

At some point a soldier in the Lord's army needs to be trusted, to be released to engage the battle in the arena of the war God has prepared them for. Submission does play an important part in that preparation but the drill sergeant then must relinquish his authority to the general (the Lord) who determines where and how you will engage the enemy or serve your fellow troops.

Servant leaders

A leader is supposed to be a servant, not a dictator, a servant preparing others to fight. This is a principle Jesus, the King of Glory, made quite clear when he washed the feet of the disciples just before he was arrested. He was arrested because he was despised and feared by those who were supposed to lead but instead demanded full control over those in their care. An issue Jesus confronted them over, time and again.

And this is what Peter was echoing when he admonished the elders in the fledgling church to not lord it over those who were seeking to learn the ways of the Lord. He was warning the leaders of the early church not to become like the Pharisees and priests, who had put burdens on people's backs that they themselves could not even bear.

> "Be shepherds of God's flock that is under your care, watching over them—not because you must, but because you are willing, as God wants you to be; not pursuing dishonest gain, but eager to serve; not lording it over those entrusted to you, but being examples to the flock" (1 Peter 5:2–3).

How did Jesus lead? By example, and by pointing people to his Father. He cared about what was going on inside of those who looked to him for *truth*, and he loved them, loved them so much that they emulated his lifestyle both during and after his time on earth. People submitted to his love, thus they listened to his Word and followed his example.

The *specifics* of what they were supposed to do would come later when he sent the *Counselor*, his Holy Spirit, to lead them where they should go and to teach them what they should say. Then he appointed and gifted leaders to teach people how to discern that Spirit, to help keep them from being led astray by false teachers and the world, by teaching them the Word. That is what we are supposed to submit to, the Word that is taught, not the specifics of what the teacher (pastor or leader) thinks you must do. The teacher might have a word for you from the Spirit or they may have a correction for you from the Spirit, but the teacher's primary task is to teach you the Word and allow you—encourage and release you—to follow Jesus. To follow Jesus into the will of the Father for *your* life.

Let's back up a bit in Hebrews 13 where we found one of our earlier referenced *submit* verses:

> "Remember your leaders, who spoke the word of God to you. Consider the outcome of their way of life and imitate their faith. Jesus Christ is the same yesterday and today and forever. Do not be carried away by all

kinds of strange teachings. It is good for our hearts to be strengthened by grace . . ." (Heb. 13:7–9).

If you take a close look here, you will discern that there are high expectations for a leader who is worthy of submission. He or she must be speaking the Word of God, not just what they feel is right today or what best serves their own purposes. They must have a life that bears evidence that they live what they teach. The "Do as I say, not as I do" principle will not fly here. They must keep Jesus central to their teaching, Jesus as unchanging— "the same yesterday and today and forever" (Heb. 13:8) Jesus that we find in the Holy Scriptures. That's not a random phrase just thrown into the middle of a scriptural leadership discussion because it sounds good. It is the key to everything a leader in the church is and does. A leader worthy of submission is not getting distracted by the latest and greatest teaching coming down the pike but is always hanging on to the heart-strengthening message of grace. As we just read: "Do not be carried away by all kinds of strange teachings. It is good for our hearts to be strengthened by grace. . . ."

The rest of that verse we looked at in Hebrews earlier that is often thrown at us like a weapon without context: The leader worthy of submission must be watching over those who are trusting his or her teaching as one who will have to answer for how their teaching affected you—"Have confidence in your leaders and submit to their authority, because they keep watch over you as those who must give an account" (Heb. 13:17).

Any leader we are asked by God to submit to must be worthy—by merit of their concern for you and by their willingness to answer to the question— "Just who are you making disciples of?" Leadership is not something anyone should aspire to unless they are sure they are first *gifted*, and then *called*, to lead. For indeed, heavy is the head that wears the crown. And he who is first will be last and a servant of all. And our submission to a leader is not something we should be willing to give unless we are sure that the one leading us does fit that criterion and has been called to lead you at *this* time and at *this* place in your life.

You must discern

Hope Chapel Red Lodge exists because I had to decide which voice to listen to while I was spiritually hanging off the side of a mountain just like I was on that big D-8 Cat so many years ago. On the one hand, I had a leader I loved and respected—a division superintendent—signaling me from a distance that it was indeed time to move into a different season of ministry, one I knew the Lord had called me to—pastoring my own church. And on the other hand, I had a leader whom I had respected and submitted to for years, in essence, beating on my shoulder and screaming in my ear "We're gonna die!"—two very different perspectives, two very different messages.

But my bubble was telling me that I had to listen to the quieter voice, the one that could see the bigger picture, even though it might not seem safe to those adamantly telling me otherwise. I had to listen, submit to that quiet voice inside telling me what was right, who I needed to listen to, and who I needed to stop listening to. That is why I am now pastor of a church I planted—because I was too aggressive to remain an apprentice, so I went out as a journeyman.

How's your apprenticeship program coming? Who is keeping you from obeying the truth?

"You were running a good race. Who cut in on you to keep you from obeying the truth? That kind of persuasion does not come from the one who calls you. 'A little yeast works through the whole batch of dough.' I am confident in the Lord that you will take no other view. The one who is throwing you into confusion, whoever that may be, will have to pay the penalty" (Gal. 5:7–10).

There is little confusion; in fact, things become quite clear, if we submit to *the Lord* first and foremost and then, and only then, to those over you whom you believe are also listening to him. Ultimately, we are all responsible for our own actions because the Counselor is always there to show us the way and our hearts will always know what is right—if we dare to listen and to obey the *still small voice*.

Conclusion

Kingdom barbarians, be careful whom you submit to, and don't give your oath lightly. If your spiritual shepherd is not leading you closer to the Chief Shepherd and his plan for you, you may have to answer to the question: "Why did you not follow when I called, just whom did you submit to?"

My soul, my sword, and my service for my King. The kingdom needs barbarians; the kingdom needs you. In the Viking longship, everyone who has pulled an oar gets to storm the beach and get a share of the plunder. The treasures of the kingdom await you.

Skol! and God bless you, my fellow barbarians.

⮜ AFTERWORD ⮞

GONE VIKING

If you, even you, had only known on this day what
would bring you peace—but now it is hidden from your eyes. (Luke
19:42)

IF YOU HAVE made it this far—stuck it out with me—to
the end of this book, then you are ready to hear the rest of the story (at
least the beginning of the story) of how it began that I embraced the
inner barbarian, or as I have come to call it lately, "gone Viking." This
involves a close encounter with the Lord in which I became aware of his
extreme pain and concern for the current state of the church.

If you have gotten to this point in this narrative, then it will not
shock you or rock your theological boat too greatly when I recount
in the paragraphs ahead what I *heard* from the Lord. The best way to
describe it is that words are put on my heart that make it to my brain,
bypassing my ears. I say heart because feelings, or impressions, often
speak louder than the words that form around them. I often say it is
really hard to put into adequate words the things the Lord does in
your spirit, but then, that is the job of a teaching pastor, or an author,

who seeks to speak truth for the Lord. And lest there be any doubt by now when you consider how much Scripture there is in this writing, I carefully weigh everything against the written Word of God, especially before I endeavor to write or speak as an ordained minister of the gospel of Jesus Christ. "But the Advocate, the Holy Spirit, whom the Father will send in my name, will teach you all things and will remind you of everything I have said to you" (John 14:26).

So with that brief but hopefully helpful synopsis of my thoughts on how the Advocate leads me in my walk with the Lord, we will venture forth with how I was led to this ministry of what I believe is the Lord freeing his church to be the church, even if it means going Viking.

I want to start by looking at a prayer from Jesus, a prayer that, in the book of Luke where it is also recorded word for word just as it is here in Matthew, we learn comes on the heels of the return of the seventy-two disciples he had sent out to the towns of Galilee to tell people about him and his mission of healing and reconciliation to his Father. In both gospel accounts of the exchange leading up to this prayer, Jesus expresses his frustration, sadness, or anger, however you want to describe it, over the refusal to listen to and accept the message and receive the deliverance being offered. "Woe to you, Chorazin! Woe to you, Bethsaida! For if the mighty works which were done in you had been done in Tyre and Sidon, they would have repented long ago in sackcloth and ashes" (Matt. 11:21 NKJV).

He then rejoiced and even burst into a spontaneous prayer of thanks and praise for those who were faithful to deliver that message and their excitement at seeing what God did for all those who did receive and believe. "*In that hour Jesus rejoiced in the Spirit and said,* 'I thank You, Father, Lord of heaven and earth, that You have hidden these things'" (Luke 10:21 NKJV, emphasis added).

So with that understanding of the mindset that Jesus is in, frustration on the one hand with those who missed the boat, yet overcome with joy for, and with, those who got to be used in such an amazing way—"Lord, even the demons are submit to us in your name!" (Luke 10:17)—let's read his prayer.

> At that time Jesus answered and said, "I thank You, Father, Lord of heaven and earth, that You have hidden these things from the wise and prudent and have revealed them to babes. Even so, Father, for so it seemed good in Your sight. All things have been delivered to Me by My Father, and no one knows the Son except the Father. Nor does anyone know the Father except the Son, and the one to whom the Son wills to reveal Him. Come to Me, all you who labor and are heavy laden, and I will give you rest. Take My yoke upon you and learn from Me, for I am gentle and lowly in heart, and you will find rest for your souls. For My yoke is easy and My burden is light." (Matt. 11:25–30 NKJV)

Here we find the familiar words of Jesus, "Take my yoke upon you and learn from me for My yoke is easy and My burden is light."

Jesus is rejoicing. Jesus is praying out loud, publicly, to his Father and he concludes his prayer of thanks—"Thanks for revealing yourself to these common working men and women. Thanks for showing them that all things are given to me by you, even the knowledge of who you are so that I can reveal you to them through their knowledge of me"—he concludes his prayer by stating, from his Father and for his Father—he's praying, yet he is giving us a message at the same time, what we would call prophesying—that we need to "come to him" and "learn from him" so that our burdens will be light and we can find rest for our souls.

I don't know, it seems kind of confusing and even contradictory to me. "*Woe* to all you cities who refused to listen to those who worked so hard to bring you the news; yay for all you who went off with nothing but a story and came back with nothing but a story; let's go tell the rest of the people in the land, and by the way, this is all easy, right, my yoke and my burden?" In a fit of honesty we would all say, "No, it's not!"

Minion minded

That's because we, the church, have missed it. I have been trying to teach my church for the last seven years and model our ministry based on this principle, that if we are doing what we are supposed to be doing, what we are passionate about and anointed to do, just like Jesus is (and now the seventy-two), we will find joy, and serving Jesus will not be a burden. And if we are doing it in his strength, when he asks, and for as long as he asks, it won't be a yoke we cannot bear, and in fact will even be like rest. If we are doing our God-given tasks in his strength, we are not depleting our own—it's that simple.

But few of us do that. I don't care if you are the pastor of the biggest church in town or the newest believer in the smallest church in town, few people in the church today are truly doing what the Lord has asked, are truly ministering, loving, and serving in *his* strength, heeding *his* voice, and reporting back to him so he can celebrate with us. So we are tired, the church is tired, and Jesus is not rejoicing in that. Jesus is *gentle and lowly in heart* and yet we are afraid to stop long enough to sit at his feet and listen, afraid we might get in trouble for stopping, we might hear something we don't like, or we just really don't believe we will, or can, hear anything.

So we look to others. "What do you want me to do? Lead me, push me, teach me. . . . " and we subject ourselves to leaders who would take advantage of our willingness to serve and to submit, and we even become those leaders ourselves because . . . the only way to stop being a lowly minion is to have our own minions. You know what that gets you? A lot of needy and eventually resentful minions. Until you get so frustrated and tired from trying to corral your minions that you throw up your hands and walk away, without even going to the Lord and asking: "What did I miss? My yoke is far from easy and my burden is far from light!"

If you did go to the Lord and ask, you would see that the Lord is not rejoicing. In fact, he is weeping—weeping over his church. He didn't want tired minions; he wanted children, friends, people who would serve with him, and through him, and side by side with others who love him and have been called according to his purpose.

> "Whoever listens to you listens to me; whoever rejects you rejects me; but whoever rejects me rejects him who sent me. The seventy-two returned with joy and said, 'Lord, even the demons submit to us in your name'" (Luke 10:16–17 NKJV).

"Whoever listens to you listens to me." That doesn't happen unless we know what it is the Lord wants us to say, and we don't know what the Lord wants us to say unless we are anointed, unless we are called and sent—by him and him alone—with our brothers and sisters in arms, equals, *babes,* who have things revealed to us that the wise and learned missed in all their arrogant bluster and busyness.

Jesus weeps

Jesus weeps for his bride, just as he did for those he first came for, the bride who rejected him because they were too busy serving the God in their scrolls and in their grand temple to recognize that he had come to them in their Holy City, on a donkey just as their scrolls had said he would. They were too busy clinging to a history to recognize the God in their present. They rejected their peace, they forsook their rest, their books were complete. "God no longer speaks, we just need to defend our religion and justify our positions—'Work, work, work—you despicable minions!'"

This attitude broke the heart of the Lord. "He saw the city and wept over it, saying, 'If you had known, even you, especially in this your day, the things that make for your peace!'" (Luke 19:41–42 NKJV).

So all that to set the stage for the part where I am going to tell you why I went Viking, why I *had* to go Viking to get to Red Lodge where I started the ministry that birthed this book. In other words, why I embraced my inner barbarian and harnessed him for God. It was a process and it took a while to get me to that point. I did not want to go Viking, far from it. I liked being part of a well-organized army. I didn't want to have to break away from that structure—"Tell me how high to jump and where to jump and let's kick some devil butt."

But I came to realize that too many soldiers were getting left behind, there were no weekend passes for R&R, and our wounded were shot and left behind where they lay with a "tsk tsk" and a "There but by the grace of God go I— too bad, they seemed to have such promise." I had to do something different, to break the ties that bind. And that is the original meaning of going "Viking"— to go rogue, raiding and conquering, a band of free men breaking away on their own to raid and conquer. It often wasn't considered a good thing by those who stayed behind and played by the rules, at least not until they saw the rewards.

We have come to associate Viking with a people group—the Norsemen who swooped down from the frozen north and for a time threatened to conquer and colonize most of the known world, but it is actually a verb. So when I say *I went Viking*, it means I jumped ship and found my own ship, one not led by a man but one led by the Son, S-o-n. With my sails full and my sun stone to guide me, I left the regiment I had been serving in and struck out to find the battle that I was being called and compelled to join.

It's a long story, and one for another time, but I was coerced by the Holy Spirit in 2001 to take classes at the Yellowstone Valley Bible Institute in Billings. I say coerced because I didn't really want to, knowing that the intent of the Lord was to make me a pastor. But the Lord would not let me have any real peace until I answered the call. So after I signed up, the Lord did some more work on my heart and got me to a place where I stopped dragging my feet and fully embraced my call. "If the God of the universe wants me to do something, who am I to argue?"

Planting

Well, long story short, two years into my classes I decided, with the blessing of the Lord, to help start a church on the south side of Billings. I jumped into that with both feet and was asked to head up the kids' ministry there. So with a year's worth of classes left at the Bible institute, while still working full-time construction (as I still am at the time of this writing) and raising three girls, I built a kids' ministry from the ground up in a church that quickly grew to a couple of hundred people.

About a year in, and after finishing my schooling, I decided, with a lot of encouragement from the pastor, to start a Wednesday evening kids' program also. We even bought a bus to haul kids in. So besides recruiting and being responsible for dozens of teachers and nursery workers, I also led worship for the kids and always had an object lesson for them, twice on Sunday and then on Wednesday evening.

Then I took on organizing VBSs, kids camps, designing and remodeling a new church building, and I taught and led worship once a month for *Celebrate Recovery*, did counseling and an occasional wedding, always seemed to find myself leading another Bible study or helping organize another event—I threw everything into that church for seven years, getting people saved and hoping and praying that soon my hard work would pay off and I wouldn't have to keep working construction to pay the bills, that I could get a paycheck from the church that matched the work I was doing there.

Instead, I got exhausted. We did a lot of wonderful things, bore a lot of fruit, and my girls were growing up and were a big part of the church, which was a good thing because they didn't see much of me outside of the church. I was actually struggling with the mindset—implied and exemplified, by those whom I looked to as examples and leaders—that family was a hindrance to the work of the kingdom, unless of course, they were as involved, enthusiastic, and tireless as you were.

Turns out I wasn't tireless, and my enthusiasm was waning. When the blown discs in my back caused by an accident at work when I fell seventeen feet from a ladder, finally got to the point where the pain was unbearable and I required another major surgery to correct it, I was relieved. I was not relieved that I was going to finally, hopefully, get this fixed—I was looking at a fusion of three vertebrae in my lower back with no guarantees that I would even get any relief. What I was relieved about was that finally, I was going to have an excuse to rest, to take a break.

Forced rest

I was actually looking forward to a major and very painful surgery, one that would require four months of recovery, wearing a back brace while the bones fused together. I was looking forward to just stopping, getting away from the church that had required every spare moment and ounce of energy I could muster—"I've got to do this, I've got to be here, this person is counting on me, that person is expecting me, if I let up the ministry will diminish, people will leave, and I'll never get to be full time, the leadership will blame me for declining attendance—the Lord will be disappointed—people will go to hell and *I will spend eternity regretting not doing more!"*

"Slap me on the table, Doc, and cut me open. Let's get this done, I have a city to save!" So I told my humble worship assistant, Rick, who was just starting to figure out how to play his guitar and sing at the same time (he is now the very capable and anointed worship leader at our church, Hope Chapel Red Lodge), that he was in charge of kids worship for the next several weeks—and I went under the knife.

Gone Viking

They cut open my stomach to get to the front part of my spine and they cut open my back to get a chunk of bone from my hip for the fusion, and after a few days in the hospital they sent me home to recover. Needless to say, I was in a lot of pain. I planted myself in a recliner and watched a lot of movies. I slept in that recliner for a few weeks because it hurt too much to lie down and I could only get up with a walker—but hey, I was getting finally getting a break! No one was counting on me to be anywhere. No one was expecting me to be there for them, to fix this, to plan that, to support or facilitate anything.

But I had given myself an assignment even so. I had been wanting to write my daughters a letter, telling them how much I loved them and explaining why I was passionate about the Lord and just how much the Lord loved them as well. I had purchased a blank journal and a brand-new gel pen just for this occasion. I knew I would be too sore to sit at the computer so I sat there in that recliner and wrote it out longhand. I wrote until the pen ran out of ink and a few months later was finally able to type it up on the computer so I could print it off and give it to my girls.

It would later become my first book, aptly entitled *To My Girls*. If that had been the only thing that came out of that forced convalescence, that would have been a lot as that letter touched not just my daughters, but many others as well. But the Lord was also using this time to speak to me about something else. The Holy Spirit was putting something in my heart, pestering me if you will, about something that I would not have come up with on my own, something I did not really want to do, and that was to pull up stakes, leave the big city and the church I had worked so hard to build, and go to the little town of Red Lodge, Montana, to start a church. *What? Why?*

It wasn't that I had anything against Red Lodge. It is a beautiful and historic little town (a tourist town) at the foot of the Beartooth Mountains. Donna and I had both spent a lot of time here, either passing through on the way to fishing or camping in mountains, on the way to Yellowstone Park, or just going there for a day to get away. But to start a church there?

"Lord, can't I go to a big town somewhere, someplace where I can build a church big enough to support me? Besides, you told me years ago that Billings was my mission field."

I would have this discussion with the Lord when I was shuffling down the dirt road near our home with the snowcapped Beartooth Mountains gleaming in the distance—getting my required walking in as part of my recovery from surgery.

So after a month or two, when I was able to get around better, I drove up to the top of the Rimrocks (the yellow sandstone cliffs that create the valley Billings sits in) looking over Billings, to do a little serious praying. I went there because in 1985 the Lord had taken me there in a vision and told me that Billings was my mission field, so if the Lord was going to tell me to leave there, it was going to have to be while I was overlooking the city I loved, the city still full of a lot of people who needed to be saved.

Well, the Lord met me there in a big way, and we had quite a conversation, one that would change my life forever. First, he told me that I was released from Billings, that I had fulfilled my obligation to save the city by helping raise up a generation that would do just that. I wrote in my Journal on July 2, 2007, that the Lord had told me, " . . . my task was finished there, it was time to move on." But that was just the start of the conversation I would have with the Lord that day. After praying for a while, suddenly I began to feel a heartache like I had never experienced before. I started weeping—sobbing—and I distinctly heard the Lord say to me, "My people are tired, so tired."

The Lord's sorrow

I was feeling the Lord's pain for his church, his sorrow and anguish, as he witnessed his people working, toiling, stressing, and striving to please him, to please their leaders, doing everything humanly possible to try to build his kingdom in their own strength until, in exasperation, they either fell by the wayside in shame and pain, or died exhausted, never having fulfilled their true purpose, never having taken the time to come to him, to him whose *yoke is easy and burden is light.*

He was asking me to go to Red Lodge, not to save the town, not to build a big church, but to build a sanctuary, a refuge, where people could come from all around and rediscover what it means to follow the one they first fell in love with—*Jesus Christ.* A place, as he put it and as I also recorded in my journal, "where the wounded and tired could go to be strengthened and built up." I can't even begin to explain what happened in my heart at that moment. The intensity of that moment, that brief but intense glimpse of the Lord's pain, put in my heart a passion that overrode every other passion and drive that I had to that point.

I was an evangelist, I was a teacher, and I was a worship leader. I was becoming an expert at how to do church and do it well. I was a minion with minions—but now I was being told that we were all working ourselves right out of the peace he offered, that we were striving so hard for—and *I* was supposed to do something about it? There was no way I was going to refuse, no matter the road ahead. "He saw the city and wept over it, saying, 'If you had known, even you, [—church—], especially in this your day, the things that make for your peace!'" (Luke 19:41–42 NKJV).

"Jesus Christ is the same yesterday, today, and forever" (Heb. 13:8). The things that broke his heart then break his heart today. We toil and strive but we stop learning from him and content ourselves to learn about him and end up striving to please a God who is recorded in our scrolls, our Bibles, while neglecting the relationship that same book tells us, *begs* us, to have with him. Thus we have no rest, and we have no peace.

> "Come to Me, all you who labor and are heavy laden, and I will give you rest. Take My yoke upon you and learn from Me, for I am gentle and lowly in heart, and you will find rest for your souls. For My yoke is easy and My burden is light" (Matt. 11:28–30 NKJV).

So after my time spent with the Lord atop the rims, I was ready to go conquer Red Lodge and build the sanctuary he spoke of. But I still had a few things to learn. The Lord told me through someone I knew to be prophetically gifted, whom I had asked to pray for me shortly after my rim top experience that "There was something he (I) needed to do first." I now know that he needed to teach me some of what *we* were doing wrong, so I wouldn't just continue the *manic cycle*—just in a prettier place.

I now believe that "that something I needed to do first" before I was ready to go, was to open my eyes to how we, me included, were wounding our soldiers. I began to see the church through different eyes. I began to perceive and recognize the anguish that was being carried by those who were zealous to serve but could find no balance, support, or rest. I saw how people, including myself, were being manipulated by a sticky combination of sweet words and subtle criticisms as I and others were guilted and shamed into doing things we wouldn't normally do.

I saw my wife devastated when those she loved and trusted turned against her when it was perceived that I was going Viking. I saw my daughter being ostracized and shamed when she needed the church the most. I saw church leaders, pastors, youth and kids' workers, burning out and being shamed and forgotten, mentioned only in passing as those to be pitied because they just couldn't cut it.

I saw those with a fire in their hearts for Jesus shoved back into their places and their fires quenched because those over them weren't ready to release or allow them to serve their Lord as they wanted, where they wanted, even if it had nothing to do with the church they were subject to, and *because* it had nothing to do with the church they were subject to. I am not just talking about the church I was in, I am talking about the evangelical and Pentecostal church in general, we who relished freedom and scorned tradition and ritual had become religious beyond recognition, perhaps even to Jesus, and vice versa.

Time to go

And then, in 2010, the Lord told me that it was time to go, and what a fight that was. I was determined to win that fight in the fullness of the grace and love of the one who called me, and leave well—to use the church phrase—but in the end, I pretty much just had to go Viking. I had to answer the call, to challenge the status quo on all levels, and I did, and it was not always pretty. But praise God I wasn't the only one going Viking. It was and continues to be a movement. God was, and is, shaking up and waking up his church. The barbarians are on the move.

A line was drawn and now my denomination as a whole, and I mean the leadership, after some major shake-ups, is crossing that line, that line between controlling the church and equipping the church. And praise God for that. But I largely stopped obsessing about what they are doing a while ago because part of going Viking, being the barbarian, meant that I had to just stop worrying about what the denomination was doing or not doing and focus on what I was doing. I am accountable to the leadership, I choose to be, but ultimately my leader is my Lord and his voice is the one that matters—in that I am finally finding peace. And it is making a dent in breaking open the cage we the church had stuffed ourselves into.

Conclusion

It's really hard to put my passion into words. Bottom line is, after feeling the Lord's anguish, hearing him weep for his church, I had to do something. I had to make a difference. I cannot stand idly by and watch the church I love suffer. I could not feel the Lord's heartache and do nothing. The Viking analogy falls short of the depth of my experience and call, but it is one that works if we understand it as a verb. To go Viking means to go and do something that is out of the norm, that goes against the establishment. It is going forth with a determination to do something and to make it happen no matter how difficult and no matter if it makes you popular. It is scary and can require great effort, sacrifice, and costs, but if successful, it can reap great rewards.

God sent me to Red Lodge specifically for the mission of building a safe place for his soldiers, and he did that because he knew that there would be others there with the heart of a barbarian who would help me build the ministry he called me to build. We have been doing that, but I know we have a long way to go. There are still a lot of wounded soldiers out there who need "Healing, Restoration, and Hope," the three principles our ministry is called to facilitate.

I now feel the Lord's joy in the victories we win there. It's not about crowds of nameless people raising their hands at an invitation who, if they come back, are then pounced on to join and serve. It's not how many seats we can fill. For me, in this season, it's about making a real difference in the heart of a person, seeing with the eyes of Jesus the heart and the hurt behind the mask. It's giving the Viking, *the barbarian*, a place to call home.

That's the burden and the yoke I chose to bear, and in that, against all reason, my soul has found rest.

May you find his rest also, my brothers and sisters in arms.

Rev. Dan Swaningson

Hope Chapel, Red Lodge Foursquare Church

ORDER INFORMATION

REDEMPTION PRESS

To order additional copies of this book, please visit
www.redemption-press.com.
Also available on Amazon.com and BarnesandNoble.com
Or by calling toll free 1-844-2REDEEM.

CPSIA information can be obtained
at www.ICGtesting.com
Printed in the USA
FSHW04n0912170418
46860FS

9 781683 144762